Tanganyikan guerrilla: East African campaign 1914-18

Pan/Ballantine

Tanganyikan guerrilla: East African campaign 1914-18

Major J R Sibley

Editor-in-Chief: Barrie Pitt
Editor: David Mason
Art Director: Sarah Kingham
Picture Editor: Robert Hunt
Designer: Barry Miles
Cover: Denis Piper
Special Drawings: John Batchelor
Photographic Research: Jasmine Spencer
Cartographer: Richard Natkiel

Photographs for this book were specially selected from the following Archives: from left to right pages: 2–3 Bundesarchiv; 6 Ullstein; 8–9 Imperial War Museum; 11 Ullstein; 13 Bundesarchiv; 16 Bundesarchiv; 17 Ullstein; 19–22 Bundesarchiv; 23 Ullstein; 24–5 Bundesarchiv; 27 T E Stepney; 29 Bundesarchiv; 30–1 Ullstein; 32–5 Bundesarchiv; 35 Ullstein; 35 Bundesarchiv; 36–7 Pictorial Press; 41 Bayer Haupstaatsarchiv Munchen; 42–3 Bundesarchiv; 44 Pictorial Press; 45 Public Records Office, London; 47 Bundesarchiv; 48–9 IWM; 51 Public Records Office; 52–5 Pictorial Press; 56 Public Records Office; 57 Ullstein; 58 IWM; 59 Public Records Office; 59–63 IWM; 64–5 Bundesarchiv; 66–7 IWM; 68 Bundesarchiv; 72 IWM; 73–76 Bundesarchiv; 77–83 IWM; 84–5 Bundesarchiv; 87 IWM; 89 Pictorial Press; 91–3 IWM; 94–5 Public Records Office; 97–100 IWM; 101 Bundesarchiv; 103–6 IWM; 107–110 Public Records Office; 112–3 Bundesarchiv; 114–5 IWM; 117 Bundesarchiv; 118 Haupstaatsarchiv; 120 Pictorial Press; 120–135 IWM; 136–7 Bundesarchiv; 138 Haupstaatsarchiv; 145 Radio-Times Hulton Picture Library; 145–9 Bundesarchiv; 151 IWM; 152 Bundesarchiv; 153 Ullstein; 154–5 Bundesarchiv; 156–8 IWM; 159 Bundesarchiv; Front Cover: Haupstaatsarchiv; Back Cover: Ullstein

ISBN 0 345 09801 3

First published in the United States 1971
This Pan/Ballantine edition published 1973 by
Pan Books Ltd, 33 Tothill Street, London SW1

Printed Offset Litho in Great Britain by
Cox & Wyman Ltd, London, Fakenham and Reading

Contents

Classic campaign

Introduction by Barrie Pitt

The campaign fought in East Africa from 1914 to 1918 was the antithesis of the conflict then taking place on the Western Front. In Europe the war was a static affair of bludgeoning, set-piece attacks with the advantage lying mainly with the defender; in East Africa it was a fluid war of movement, in which, generally speaking, the advantage lay with the attacker. Unlike the Western Front where commanders on both sides tended to be remote from their troops, directing the battle from headquarters situated well back from the front line, in East Africa – certainly from the time when Lieutenant-General Smuts took command of the British forces – the commanders were more personally involved and shared many of the hardships of their men. The conduct of the East African campaign, perhaps more than any other throughout the war, was influenced by the personality of one man.

Paul von Lettow Vorbeck was, at the outbreak of war, a lieutenant-colonel in command of the forces of the protectorate of German East Africa; he was a veteran of the Boxer rebellion of 1900–01 and the Herero campaign in South West Africa of 1904–06, in which he had observed and assimilated the techniques of guerrilla warfare – techniques he was to put effectively into practice during the next four years. The force he com-

manded consisted, in 1914, of 260 Germans and approximately 2,472 askaris, or native soldiers, organised into companies, each company a self-contained mobile tactical unit.

When war began, Lettow Vorbeck determined to do all in his power to disrupt the Allied war effort; it was his declared intention to pose sufficient threat to British interests in East Africa to force the British to divert troops from other, more important, theatres of operations. That he was able to achieve his aims so successfully says much for his ability as a leader of men and for his tactical and strategic skill; in four years' campaigning he avoided commitment to any major battle and by the end of the war had cost Britain dear in both men and materials.

The German forces had a persistent quality about them which defied all efforts made to force them into a pitched battle, or to deprive them of essential supplies. The same quality seemed to attach itself to the *Königs-*

berg, the German cruiser which sank *HMS Pegasus* in Zanzibar harbour and sought refuge in the dense jungle of the Rufiji river delta, where she was eventually sunk by two Royal Navy monitors. The once sleek grey cruiser, terror of the shipping lanes, though battered and rusting away in the muddy waters of an African creek, fought on through those of her guns which were removed and continued the war with Lettow Vorbeck's will-o'-the-wisp *Schutztruppen*.

From the British point of view, the war in East Africa was notable for the amount of effort which had to be expended to achieve often limited objectives. In the affair of the *Königsberg* which the Admiralty had treated as top priority, two monitors had to be sent all the way from Malta to the Rufiji delta; a civilian flying boat was purchased by the navy from Durban and its pilot given a temporary commission so that he might fly the aircraft on reconnaissance flights to locate exactly the elusive German cruiser. To Lake Tanganyika, where the Germans had three gunboats, the British brought two motor gunboats from England, transporting them in sections by sea to Capetown and thence overland by rail and bush trail to the lake where they were re-assembled and promptly established Britannia's proper dominance over the waves of this inland sea.

At the beginning of the war, as soon as Lettow Vorbeck's aggressive intentions were realised, the British quickly sent two expeditionary forces to East Africa from India; one to reinforce the King's African Rifles who had opposed the early German moves, and the second to invade German East Africa. It was this second expeditionary force, composed of poor quality troops, recently re-armed with standard short Lee-Enfield rifles – weapons with which they were not familiar – which attempted the landing at Tanga on 2nd November, 1914. Disregarding every basic principle of warfare, the Battle of Tanga was, for the British, a shameful fiasco which boosted the morale of the German troops and provided many of them with modern rifles and other military equipment abandoned on the beaches by panic-stricken Indian soldiers.

When Lieutenant-General Jan Smuts took over command in 1915, fresh from his successes with General Botha against the Germans in South West Africa, the British forces immediately began a more purposeful and aggressive campaign: but despite Smuts' leadership and enterprise, and the determined pursuit of the German columns by his successor van Deventer, at no time was the German force seriously threatened.

Paul von Lettow Vorbeck remained in command of the German East African army until after the Armistice was signed. He surrendered undefeated, and in recognition of their bravery, van Deventer allowed the officers and European other ranks to retain their arms. At a formal surrender ceremony at Abercorn on 25th November, 1918, there ended what must surely be one of the finest feats of generalship in modern times. The bulk of Lettow Vorbeck's troops were African askaris fighting in a war of European origin which they could not understand; they had no patriotic fervour to help them overcome the rigours and hardships of this arduous campaign and for several years they were cut off from the outside world and became, perforce, completely self-reliant. Throughout this time their commander managed to maintain the morale of his troops and controlled the complex movements of independent companies without benefit of such aids to communication as are available to military commanders today.

This little-known, four-year long campaign in which a small force tied down an army many times larger than itself, remains a classic example of what can be accomplished in a guerrilla war by well-led, disciplined troops.

Prelude to war

In the annals of the First World War, this little known campaign fought mainly in German East Africa was unique, for the colony continued to be a battlefield throughout the entire four years of the struggle, remaining undefeated to the end. General Paul von Lettow Vorbeck, the commander of the German colonial force, was never overcome, and surrendered only after the Armistice had been signed. His tiny army was never decisively defeated by the British, and throughout he fought a guerrilla campaign and a fighting withdrawal which forced the British to maintain in East Africa an army equivalent in size to the force which had been needed to defeat the Boers in the South African War.

In the scramble for Africa, which was marked by the Anglo-German agreement of July 1885, Germany had acquired an area of land nearly as big as France and Germany together. Lying a few degrees south of the equator and sandwiched between the Indian Ocean on its eastern coastline and Lakes Kivu and Tanganyika straddling its western borders, German East Africa was to present an outsize arena of 384,000

Lieutenant-General Paul von Lettow Vorbeck (second from right) with officers of the German *Schutztruppe* (defence force) and friends in German East Africa in the balmy days before the First World War

square miles for the contenders in the world conflict. A good proportion of the native population was concentrated along the flat coastal strip which widened towards the south of the colony towards the delta of the River Ruvuma. Inland, the ground rose gradually to 3,000 feet and the central plateau. Here the scene was one of vast distances of waterless thorn scrub in the centre of the territory. Progressing north-east in the direction of British East Africa where the water-table was higher, it took on the appearance of open parkland and savannah where game abounded. Lake Victoria in the north was ringed by the lush vegetation more usually associated with equatorial regions. In the south were the southern highlands around Iringa and Neu Langenberg, the former to be later the centre of profitable tea plantations. As the land dropped again vast tracts of bare, uninviting land, impassable during the rainy season, took the place of the fertile green of the higher slopes.

The main mountain features lay in the north-east of the territory: the single snow-capped peak of Kilimanjaro and the Usambara and Pare range towards the coast at Tanga. The Great Rift Valley, the tremendous geographical split which begins in Syria and continues into the continent of Africa via the Red Sea, divides East Africa from north to south. In some parts it is 400 miles wide and 2,000 feet deep. It rises to 8,000 feet above sea level, and around its course the vegetation turns to tropical forest. The boundary line between British and German spheres of influence, that is, British East Africa (now Kenya) and Uganda in the north, and German East Africa (now the mainland of Tanzania) in the south, was an arbitrary line drawn on the map with little or no reference to the tribal delineations of the African population or even the natural features of the area. The well-known story of the gift of Mount Kilimanjaro by Queen Victoria to the Kaiser a few

years later (rumoured to be because he had no high snow-clad peak in his empire) is perhaps indicative of the rather flippant attitude of the then imperial rulers and their governments towards the frontier lines of their overseas possessions.

Thus many features, both physical and climatic, made German East Africa an area of war completely different from Europe's Western Front. There were wide variations in climate, from the sweltering damp heat of the coastal belt around Dar es Salaam and Tanga, to the fierce sun and penetrating dust of the dry central plateau. There were the cold mists of the highlands near Moshi and in the foothills of Kilimanjaro, as well as near Iringa in the Sao Hill area further south.

The campaign was fought mostly in 'bush' country, which in fact was anything from open parkland to dense forest or thorn scrub. Such country was bound to be an obstacle to successful military operations. These physical and climatic hazards were quite arduous enough, but coupled with the dangers of rhinoceros, elephant, lion and crocodile, command and control became formidable tasks. Then there were the minutiae of such tropical regions with which the soldier had to contend: the constant battle against mosquitoes, tsetse flies, jiggers and ticks, and the host of tropical diseases which accompany them (including malaria and sleeping sickness), not to mention bilharzia from infected rivers and lakes. It followed

Top: The topography of German East Africa, Germany's prize colony, varied widely, from savannah, to scrub-covered plateau, to mountains, and to tropical forest, but generally it was unsuitable for conventional European warfare.
Right: The prewar development of the colony – the construction of the Dar es Salaam railway which by 1914 ran right across the colony from Dar on the coast to Kigoma on Lake Tanganyika

that the health problem would be great. The scorpions, warrior ants and wild bees were ever present.

Furthermore, in contrast with other theatres of war, where vast armies operated in small areas both in Europe and the Middle East without any great degree of mobility, the fighting in East Africa presented the picture of small mobile forces operating over vast distances of the African continent.

The commander in any theatre of war always has his problems, but in East Africa it can be well appreciated how the usual difficulties were magnified and augmented by the alien natural features of the country. The terrain, the lack of adequate roads and sufficient transport, worked against the side that needed a quick decision. The logistical problems of obtaining food, water and a supply of ammunition were always a constant headache in East Africa, and grew as the size of the army increased. The tactics employed in France and Germany could not possibly work in German East Africa. A new system of tactics had to be evolved, particularly in regard to the relation of fire and movement and communication in difficult country. There were no accurate maps, so the problems which beset commanders were extremely testing on the tactical side. The vast distances involved made the movement of troops from one theatre of operations to another very difficult.

The Germans (working on interior lines of communication) started with an advantage. As early as 1896, the Imperial Government in Berlin had sanctioned the building of a railway line to open up the hinterland behind the port of Tanga. It had reached Moshi at the foot of Kilimanjaro by 1912. A second line, this time westwards from Dar es Salaam, was started in 1904, reaching Morogoro in 1908. It continued towards the heart of the territory, reaching Tabora (a distance of 526 miles inland) in 1912, and by 1914 its terminal had been established at Kigoma on Lake Tanganyika on the far side of the colony. The Allies had to work on exterior lines of communication, and consequently the problem of troop movement and resupply was that much more difficult.

At the outbreak of war in 1914, British East Africa and Uganda were totally unprepared for hostilities. In fact, the crisis in Europe had attracted little serious comment until the last days of July. On 29th July the telegraph from the Colonial Office to Sir Henry Belfield, the Governor of British East Africa, had stated that precautionary measures were to be put into force. From the foundation of British influence and settlement in East Africa, deliberately it may seem, no special emphasis had been placed on the establishment of a particularly strong armed force. The last decade of the 19th Century saw more of the local tribesmen recruited into the Central African Rifles, the East African Rifles and the Uganda Rifles, three regiments which had evolved from a nucleus originally enlisted in the Sudan and which were to be combined in 1902 to form the new colonial regiment on which Edward VII was pleased to confer the title 'The King's African Rifles' (KAR). From Nyasaland in the south to the borders of Abyssinia in the north, Yaos, Nandi, Kavirendo, Wanyamwezi and many others found their way into the ranks of the new regiment.

Throughout the ten years preceeding the war, companies and battalions were redistributed or dispersed throughout their regions on numerous occasions and almost, it seemed at random. There seemed to be no uniformity or planned continuity for the new regiment. The only rôle it played was that of internal security interspersed with local excursions to subjugate erring tribesmen. Thus on the eve of war this small force in British East Africa and Uganda was made up of the 3rd Battalion and 4th Battalion KAR, and four companies of the 1st Battalion KAR attached from Nyasaland. In all, this totalled seventeen small companies. Incredibly, there was no organisation existing which could expand the KAR in an emergency.

The KAR, which was to bear the brunt of most of the fighting in the initial and final stages of the war, was spread over three territories. The HQ of 3rd KAR was in Nairobi, but its five companies and its Camel Company were dispersed throughout British East Africa. HQ of 4th KAR was in Bombo, and its seven companies were dispersed in Uganda. The Governor was overall C-in-C and exercised his authority through the KAR commanding officers. This naturally led to a certain degree of friction, for the direct command of soldiers by civil administration always works out badly. On the opposing German side the order was the same and the German commander also had his problems, for he was directly under command of the Governor, Dr Schnee, who was convinced that war in German East Africa was unnecessary.

British strength at 4th August 1914 was 62 officers and 2,319 African ranks, a ratio of roughly thirty Africans to one European. The soldiers, or askaris as they were known, were African infantry soldiers carrying rifles. Each company had one machine gun, there being no artillery in this force. The lack of any organisation readily capable of expanding the KAR became supremely significant as the campaign progressed, for in the ensuing years reinforcements had to be diverted from India and elsewhere to this particular theatre of war. To speculate on this non-reinforcement of the KAR at the outset of hostilities is interesting. Like their German counterparts it is possible that the British expected the war in East Africa would not be prolonged and that the Germans and British would come to some agreement to terminate any fighting quickly. It was considered that any indication of

The *Schutztruppe* in training. Its peacetime use had so far been restricted to the quashing of tribal risings

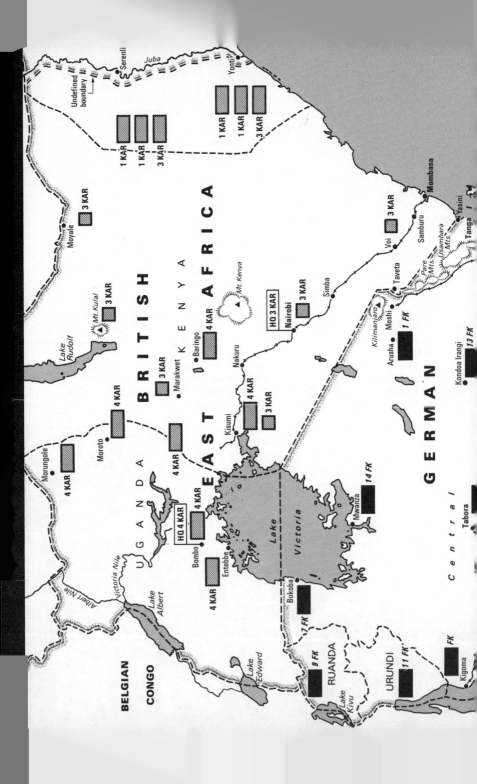

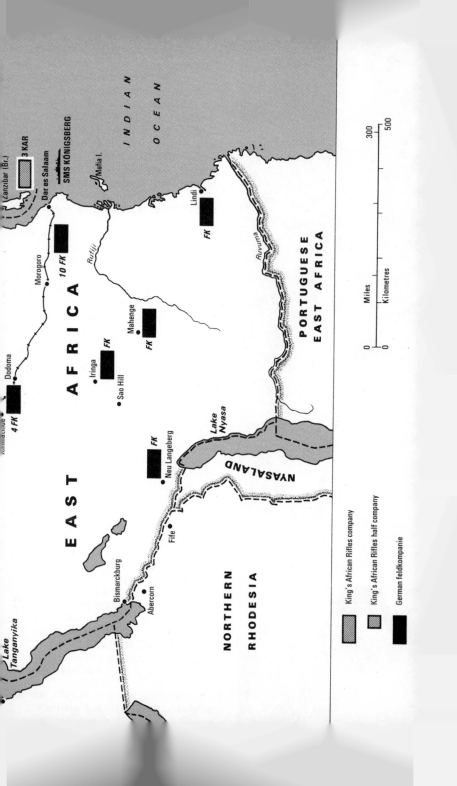

hostility between the European races would inevitably affect both their colonial positions vis-à-vis the Africans. Nonetheless there was no shortage of European volunteers to join the KAR at the beginning of the war. Nearly 3,000 came forward, but as there were no arms, no ammunition, no transport and no staff organisation, it was difficult to form them into a coherent fighting body. But a volunteer reserve was eventually set up, and the East African Mounted Rifles and the East African Regiment were formed.

The defence force of the German Protectorate (the *Schutztruppe*) was commanded by the then Lieutenant-Colonel Paul von Lettow Vorbeck, a Prussian officer who had had considerable experience in colonial and guerrilla warfare. This had been gained in China during the Boxer Revolt 1900–1901, and in South West Africa in the Herero Campaign 1904–1906 when he served on the staff of General von Trotha and as an independent company detachment commander. He had been wounded in 1906 in South West Africa and had visited German East Africa on his return to Germany. South West Africa afforded him the unique experience of soldiering in a guerrilla campaign over severe terrain. He learned many lessons from the Africans he had fought, and these were all to be put into practical effect when he took command in East Africa.

From the time of his graduation from the *Kriegschule*, where he met cadets like Tom von Prince who were later to serve with him in the East African campaign, Lettow Vorbeck seemed destined to spend most of his time in German territory abroad. His temperament and aptitudes seemed particularly suited to this turn of career. With a meticulous Prussian eye for detail, he was the ascetic type readily

Lettow Vorbeck in Berlin in 1914. He had already had successful experience of colonial and guerrilla warfare in China and South West Africa

prepared to suffer and enjoy both the hardships and bonuses of colonial soldiering.

He was adamant in his belief that the white man was in Africa to rule, to lead without any assistance from the black man, and it was his job as the military leader to enforce the policies emanating from Berlin, whatever the cost. It is not surprising, therefore, that he regarded with suspicion the liberal schemes of Dr Schnee. Once the British had shown their hand in Europe, there could be no conciliation, even thousands of miles away from the main theatres of war. He was totally against any hint of neutrality. Moreover, he had a flair for languages which was further developed in the inter-racial atmosphere of the Boxer War and was very necessary when commanding a Swahili-speaking African army. He was to become, during the four years of this war, one of the most interesting commanders in the field and, indeed, one of the few German generals who fought on after the Armistice. In fact he was never completely defeated. The strength of his character, his drive and outstanding professional ability were the major factors which impelled the Germans and their askaris to fight on for four years in the most adverse conditions without any hope of further war supplies or reinforcements. This achievement must rank as one of the outstanding feats of leadership in the First World War.

At the outbreak of the war the German forces were organised much on the same lines as the British troops. In the last decade of the 19th Century, Hermann von Wissman had led a force of European and native troops to put down the Arabs who had successfully resisted German claims to their territory on the mainland of East Africa. Like the British colonial

An askari soldier. Recruited from local tribes, askaris made up approximately ninety per cent of the *Schutztruppe*

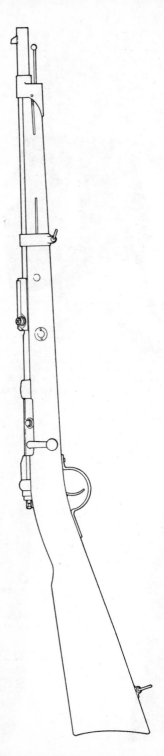

regiments of the time, he too found willing recruits in the Sudan as well as from among the Somalis. Local Swahilis (coastal Africans with a sprinkling of Arab blood) joined his force and in 1891, having fought successfully against Bushiri, the Arab leader, the Berlin government saw fit to raise Wissman's force into the *Officia Kaiserliche Schutztruppe*. It undertook both military and police functions and was steadily expanded over the next twenty years. As its operations took it from the coast inland, so the *Schutztruppe* began to recruit from subjugated tribes like the Wasukuma, the Ngoni and the Manyema. Particularly fruitful was the area around Tabora in the centre of the territory, the land of the Wanyamwezi, which produced a large proportion of the German force. It must not be forgotten also that the numbers of the *Schutztruppe* were periodically boosted by enlistment of ex-KAR soldiers who found themselves made redundant during one or other battalion reorganisation.

By 1914, the *Schutztruppe* was organised into independent regular companies, each of three platoons, each about sixty strong, giving about sixteen to twenty German officers and

The Mauser Model 1871 was the first Mauser rifle to be built in great numbers, and was a technically advanced weapon for its day, especially in the design of the action of the gun. It was an 11mm rifled weapon, firing single shots and using black powder metallic cartridges. The type was adopted by the Prussian government in 1872 and produced in their Spandau arsenal near Berlin. Although it had long been superseded by guns firing the more modern smokeless cartridges in European countries, it was still in widespread use among the world's smaller and more backward countries, and by Germany's African colonial troops in the First World War. Similar to the Model 1871 was the Model 1871/84, which featured a nine-round tubular magazine under the barrel

200 askaris. Each was a self-contained mobile tactical unit and within its organisation was a supply and transport sub-unit. These companies were either known as *Feldkompanie* (*FK*) or *Schutzenkompanie* (*SchK*). There were fourteen independent companies; overall there were 260 Germans and approximately 2,472 askaris. Each company had from two to four machine guns and also 250 carriers to carry supplies and ammunition.

As on the Western Front, the machine gun was to become the key weapon in all phases of war, advance to contact, withdrawal, defence and attack. Fighting in the bush was similar to night fighting and the results for aimed rifle fire were the same: the soldiers tended to shoot high. This was not so with the machine gun which, on a rigid base, aimed on fixed lines and produced the majority of casualties in this campaign. The 1871 pattern rifle, which used black powder, was still being used by eight of these companies, and this is a significant point because it affected the tactics employed by the askaris, for the smoke from the black powder gave away the soldiers' position. This had had little or no effect when fighting tribal wars, but in a war against more formidable opponents. it was to have repercussions on the tactical employment of troops.

There were more Europeans in a German company, about twenty German officers and NCOs, with approximately 200 askaris, making the ratio something like one European to ten Africans. Again, this is another significant factor in that it had a long term effect on the performance of the German troops during the war, particularly during difficult operations. Communications were always a difficulty in bush fighting, and the relatively large number of Europeans in the company reduced this problem.

The raw material thus assembled, Lettow Vorbeck set about the intensive training of his force. A system of tactics was evolved, and the askaris were shaped into confident fighting soldiers. Discipline and punctuality, well known Prussian characteristics, were instilled into the men. The significance of these characteristics as battle-winning factors cannot be stressed too strongly.

After intensive training and the inculcation of the Prussian virtues of discipline and punctuality the askaris were first-rate fighting men

British disaster

Lettow Vorbeck lost no time in taking the offensive. He persuaded the Governor, Dr Schnee, who still hoped that there would be no war so that his colonial development could proceed unhindered, to allow German troops to concentrate in the north of the colony. This he was loathe to do. As nominal C-in-C of the armed forces, Heinrich Schnee was to find himself in disagreement with the field commander of the *Schutztruppe* on many occasions in the coming four years. A colonial servant of some years standing, he had served in various parts of the world since he had entered the service in 1897. When he arrived in 1912, accompanied by his New Zealand wife, to undertake this prize governorship in the German Empire, he determined to pursue the benevolently liberal policies which he had formulated in dealing with other native peoples in New Guinea and Samoa.

His schemes included the expansion of medical services for the Africans, the opening of schools and the encouragement of self help in an attempt to introduce more cash crops throughout the colony. Schnee knew he needed the co-operation of chiefs and tribesmen to carry out his far-reaching schemes. Moreover he considered that geographically the colony

An Indian casualty of the abortive British landings at Tanga in November 1914

Dr Heinrich Schnee, Governor of
German East Africa and nominal C-in-C
of all the armed forces

was in a poor position to dictate any
military action and be successful
either as an aggressor or defender.
Encircled as it was by potential enemy
territory, it had a poor chance of
survival in any war. Schnee considered that he knew well enough the
unwritten rules of international behaviour, and despite the arguments of
Lettow Vorbeck, he was only too
anxious to listen to the British Consul
in Dar es Salaam.

The Agreement of 1885 had included
a neutrality clause agreed to by all
signatories. It would have been to the
distinct advantage of the British if it
had been implemented, so the British
Consul, Norman King, worked along
these lines and tried to persuade Dr
Schnee not to fight. Lettow Vorbeck,
however, had greater strategic insight
than his Governor. 'My view was that
we would best protect our colony by
threatening the enemy in his own

territory. We could very effectively
tackle him at a sensitive point, the
small forces prevent considerable
numbers of the enemy from interven-
ing in Europe. I thought we could. It
would obviously have been an advantage for England if any agreement
had existed which condemned us to
neutrality.'

The vital sector, from the stand-
point of either side, lay on the boundary of the two territories between
Mount Kilimanjaro and the sea. This
was the main area of German colonisation, but more important, either
side of the border were the two railways, the British railway linking
Uganda and Nairobi with the outside
world and the German line from
Tanga to the settled areas around
Kilimanjaro. In parts where the
British railway approached the border
it was most vulnerable, for the area
was uncultivated and uninhabited
bush. The German line was protected
by the Usambara mountain ranges
and was to some measure thus secure
from raiding parties.

Lettow Vorbeck's view was that the
Germans could best protect their
colony by threatening the British in
their own territory at the sensitive
point, the Uganda railway. This was
proved to be accurate. Vorbeck's long
term strategy was to force the British
to commit as many troops to East
Africa as possible, thus preventing
them from going to other, more
important, theatres of operation.
After he had completed his initial
tour of inspection of the colony
Lettow Vorbeck realised that communication and supply were the vital
ingredients if a successful long term
war was to be fought. Major-General
Wahle, a retired officer who was
visiting Dar es Salaam at the time,
was placed in charge of the lines of
communication.

The first German move was against
Taveta, a small post at the south-
eastern foot of Mount Kilimanjaro.
The German commander at Moshi,
Captain Tom von Prince, demanded

An African school at Kilimatinde.
Schnee was determined that his liberal
colonial policy should not suffer
because of the war, and when he tried
to arrange with the British Consul that
there should be no fighting in the colony
he came into immediate disagreement
with his field commander, Lettow
Vorbeck

that the Taveta settlement should be
evacuated. Prince himself was an
interesting character. His father was
a Scotsman, Thomas Henry Prince
who, while serving with the British
Police Force in Mauritius, had married the daughter of a German mis-
sionary out there. Orphaned at an
early age, Tom, with his sister, was
sent to live in Germany where he
attended the Ritter Akademie. Failing
to obtain a commission in the British
army, Prince entered the *Kriegschule*
at Kassel where he met his future wife,
then a girl of fourteen, the daughter
of a Prussian general. His boisterous
and wayward nature could find no
outlet within the confines of a German
military institution. Frustrated in
love (General von Massow refused to
allow him to pay court to his young
daughter, such was his reputation!),
his dual nationality came in useful,
and Prince, compelled to leave his
sweetheart behind, left the army.

It was then that Africa reclaimed
him. He found his way back to German
East Africa, rejoined the German
army and in the next few years he led
many actions to subdue the then
frequent uprisings against German
authority in the colony. His tremendous personality and reckless bravery
soon won him fame, and a grateful
Kaiser awarded him the title 'von'.
He returned to Germany a hero, and
married Magdalene von Massow, the
girl he had left behind. In 1896 they
sailed for East Africa and the next
few years followed the same pattern
as before, the dashing German officer
hunting down and subduing recal-
citrant chiefs and tribes.

Prince retired from active service
in 1900, but in 1913, farsighted enough
to see the potentially explosive situ-

A German Maxim gun emplacement in the Kilimanjaro area. Since Queen Victoria's gift of Mount Kilimanjaro to the Kaiser this area had developed into the main zone of German colonisation

ation building up in Europe, he formed a volunteer defence force among the local farmers of the Usambaras. When in 1914, after the outbreak of war, permission was relayed to him from Lettow Vorbeck to lead the first attack into British territory across the border, he was jubilant. He was at one with Lettow Vorbeck that any action in German East Africa could only help the German war effort in Europe. As the landing of the British Expeditionary Force in France was nearing completion on 15th August 1914, Colonel von Bock and Lieutenant Boell moved across the border of German East Africa and seized Taveta. The German forces attempted to exploit their success and pushed further into British territory, striking for the Uganda railway and in the direction of Mombasa. But the KAR, under the command of Colonel L E S Ward, quickly deployed to meet the German threat and, alone in the field, it prevented further incursion into British territory by its prompt action.

The Governor of British East Africa, Sir Henry Belfield, asked for reinforcements to counter the German threat. The Colonial Office turned to the India Office, which already had been asked to provide troops for the main theatres of war. The East African request was then passed to the Committee of Imperial Defence. It was decided that India should provide two Expeditionary Forces, one to capture the principal German port of Dar es Salaam, and another to reinforce the KAR. The Indian Expeditionary Force 'C', as it was to be known, was the one sent to reinforce the KAR. It comprised the 29th Punjabis, two Imperial Service battalions (made up of half-battalions from the states of Bhurtpore, Jind, Kapurthala and Rampur), 27th Mountain Battery Royal Artillery, 1st Battery of Calcutta Volunteers and one machine gun battery. This force was commanded by Brigadier-General J M Stewart, CB, ADC. Almost at the outset Lettow Vorbeck's strategic plan was succeeding!

Arriving in Mombasa on 1st September, the 29th Punjabis provided the much needed reinforcement in the Kilimanjaro area where the KAR had successfully held the German thrusts from the foothills of the mountain, at the same time subduing tribal unrest instigated by German propaganda. Lettow Vorbeck had telegraphed his commanders, 'prompt action promises quick results,' and this policy had been urged on them all. It was only by the equally prompt action of the KAR that the British Protectorate had been saved from invasion. The Germans now realised that an easy victory was impossible.

Meanwhile the other expeditionary force was assembling in Bombay after the priorities of Europe, Egypt, Persian Gulf and North West Frontier had been met. The 27th Bangalore Brigade and an Imperial Service brigade were selected to sail for East Africa. Their names are misleading as both brigades had been recruited from the length and breadth of India, both men and officers were strangers to each other and even more so to their new commanders. Command was given to Major-General Aitken, and Expeditionary Force 'B' of 8,000 men was made up of the following units: the 27th Bangalore Brigade (Commanded by Major-General R Wapshare) which comprised the 2nd Loyal North Lancashire Regiment, the 63rd Palamcottah Light Infantry, the 98th Infantry, the 101st Grenadiers, the 28th Mountain Battery RA, the 25th and 26th Companies Sappers and Miners and the 61st KGO Pioneers; the Imperial Service Brigade (Commanded by Brigadier-General M J Tighe) which comprised the 13th Rajputs, the 2nd Kashmir Rifles, a half battalion of the 3rd Kashmir Rifles, and a half battalion of the 3rd Gwalior Rifles.

The military quality of the one British battalion was unquestionable, but this could in no way be said of the Indian battalions. The 63rd and 98th had not seen active service for a generation, and this deficiency was magnified by lack of training and poor knowledge of each other. Prior to embarking, the regiments were rearmed with a standard short Lee-Enfield, which was totally new to them. Indeed, the senior staff officer, Colonel Sheppard, remarked to Major-General Aitken, after inspecting the troops at Bombay, that 'the campaign will either be a walk over or a tragedy.'

Aitken left India with Expeditionary Force 'B' on 16th October. His task was to bring the whole of German East Africa under British control by affecting a landing in Tanga and then, in conjunction with Expeditionary Force 'C', pushing forward to Moshi, the German stronghold. The comment of Captain R Meinertzhagen, an Intelligence Staff Officer on Aitken's HQ, is interesting. 'Neither am I enthusiastic about the troops sent with the force. They constitute the worst in India, and I tremble to think what may happen if we meet with serious opposition. I have seen many of the men and they did not impress me at all, either as men or as soldiers. Two battalions have no machine guns and the senior officers are nearer to fossils than active, energetic leaders of men. But it serves no useful purpose being critical at this stage. One can only hope for the best and rely on our British battalion, Mountain Battery and the element of 'surprise.'

The journey from India to Mombasa was a misery for the Indian troops of Expeditionary Force 'B'. Even physical training was a problem because their ships were so small and all available space was taken up. This

Casualties of the 13th Rajputs on the second day of the battle of Tanga, the first blow against the German colony

was particularly true of the *Assouan*, a vessel of 1,900 tons, carrying the 63rd Palamcottah Light Infantry whose subsequent poor performance at Tanga can in some measure be attributed to the rigours of the voyage.

On arrival at Mombasa, Aitken conferred with the Governor, and Tanga was settled on as the objective. The scant Intelligence that there was about the German dispositions indicated that the coastal areas were lightly held and that the German force was concentrated at Moshi. Captain Meinertzhagen, who had seen service in East Africa with the KAR, indicated that the Germans could get troops to Tanga with the greatest of ease. His advice was disregarded, as was the offer of assistance from the commanding officer of the KAR. The value of the KAR in bush warfare had not yet been recognised. Meinertzhagen recounts the fatal preparations for the imminent attack: 'Aitken's plan is to land at Tanga and then push up the Usambara railway towards Moshi, General Stewart cooperating from Voi and pushing towards Taveta. He has some 5,000 rifles and twenty machine guns. But the plan is bad, for we lay ourselves open to defeat in detail, intercommunication between the two forces being quite impossible, and secondly we would both be operating in thick bush, in terribly unhealthy country and our troops, sad to relate, are rotten.'

Again, at the conference between the Governor and Aitken, Meinertzhagen recalls the tone of the planning: 'So I spoke, giving my opinion that there was probably very little in Tanga but that there must be a large concentration in the Kilimanjaro area whence troops could be rapidly transported by rail to Tanga within thirty hours. Colonel Graham then offered to bring 3rd KAR to Mombasa at once, ship them to Tanga, and land as a covering force for our main body to disembark. I was enthusiastic as it was my old battalion, I knew they

were first class, accustomed to bush warfare and it would be a tremendous asset. But Aitken refused without a word of thanks. I was disgusted. The conference broke up very disheartened.'

For the first time Aitken was informed by Captain Caufield that the Royal Navy had previously made a truce with the Germans at Tanga and Dar es Salaam, and the Germans would have to be told if this truce were broken. The naval officers insisted, and Aitken reluctantly agreed that Tanga 'by orders from the Admiralty will have to be informed shortly before any hostile act takes place that terms of truce are not ratified'. So at one stroke, a cardinal principle of war, surprise, was sacrificed.

While the *Good Hope* and *Monmouth* were being sunk by Spee at the Battle of Coronel, the Battle of Tanga was beginning. On 2nd November Captain Caufield in HMS *Fox* steamed into Tanga to notify the abrogation of the truce. The element of surprise thrown to the wind by the British, Lettow Vorbeck at Moshi immediately despatched one-and-a-half companies down the railway to Tanga, four more companies and HQ following on 3rd November. Captain Baumstark, with two companies which were north of Tanga, was ordered to move on the town. Captain Caufield now refused to take HMS *Fox* inside the harbour for fear of mines, so minesweeping operations were begun. Aitken was therefore forced to look for other landing places and at this short notice, beaches 'A', 'B' and 'C' were selected. By this time Lettow Vorbeck had been alerted.

The war diary of the 17 *FK* indicates this clearly: 'At 11 pm the patrol over the harbour reported that two or three vessels, lighters or rowing-boats, were to be heard east of the Mission. I accordingly ordered No 3 Platoon with two machine guns to go to a house which stood on high ground, from where, helped by the bright moon, a good view could be obtained over the harbour, between the Custom

House, the Dead Island and the Mission. About midnight two enemy boats were sighted and were shot at by the machine guns evidently with good success. From one of the boats our fire was answered but only feebly and for a short time. The boats turned and went away hurriedly sending up two rockets to ask for help. As nothing happened for an hour No 3 Platoon returned and rejoined the Company. When I learnt that the enemy were making serious endeavours to land I informed our officer at Muheza so to be sure to get reinforcements by the 3rd. I was also able to telephone to HQs. and was informed that HQs and the 16th Field Company would arrive in Tanga between 5 and 6 am.'

Darkness fell quickly on the night of 2nd November. At about 2200 hours, the 13th Rajputs and 61st KGO Pioneers landed in full moonlight at Beach 'A' after wading through deep water from the lighter. Their objectives, the Red House and the Signal Tower, were

Tanga. As the British advanced through thick bush straggling occurred and the expected drill movement degenerated into an uncontrollable mob

found empty and the covering force secured its foothold, 'but the men both of the 13th and of the 61st, debilitated by nearly a month of sea sickness and cramped quarters, were thoroughly exhausted,' this according to the Official History.

The German 17 *FK*, utilizing the drainage ditch west of the railway cutting, had barricaded the three bridges over the railway cutting and constructed a defensive position in depth based on well-sited machine gun positions, the usual basis of German tactics.

The 13th and 61st advanced on Tanga township and came under very heavy fire from the German defensive position. Thus held, Brigadier-General Tighe committed his reserve, and at this moment the CO of the 13th and his Adjutant were severely wounded.

The newly-arrived German *FK*s began an enveloping movement and the British force gave way and pulled back to the Red House in great disorder.

An eye witness vividly described the battle: 'At dawn, Tighe attacked Tanga with the 13th Rajputs and the 61st Pioneers. On the edge of Tanga, Tighe ran into an entrenched position strongly held by the enemy. Soon after, he was attacked and beaten back, his' men breaking and disorganised. No amount of heroic example on behalf of the British officers availed. Officer after officer was shot down trying to rally the men and stem the tide of flight. And HMS *Fox* never fired a shot. We suffered some 300 casualties today and our men behaved disgracefully, showing no military spirit or grit. I have never had much faith in our second-rate Indian troops. Our British officers behaved like heroes but none of them had a chance with their men running like rabbits and jibbering like monkeys. By dark we had two more battalions ashore and the remainder land at daylight tomorrow. No guns are to be landed, nor Sappers, which is a pity as they have all our explosives and grenades. How easy it is to forget that military axiom, "Superiority of force at the decisive point".'

Aitken then decided that the Rajputs and Pioneers were unreliable. All troops except the gunners and sappers would be landed as soon as possible at Beaches 'B' and 'C'. No orders were given for reconnaissance, and in fact at that time Tanga was deserted, the German *FK*s having pulled back from the town. The German commander was more active than his opposite number and personally made a reconnaissance into and through Tanga on a bicycle. He also appreciated the value of artillery and in his memoirs much regretted the absence of this artillery which would have been annihilating at such close range. From his personal experiences in East Asia Lettow Vorbeck felt that British troops were moved with clumsiness in battle and he was certain that in unknown close country such as Tanga their problems would be immense.

Aitken decided to advance on 4th

November on a frontage sufficiently wide to turn the Germans' flank. The direction of the advance was to be maintained by the 2nd Loyal North Lancashire Regiment, the other less reliable battalions to be sandwiched between the best battalions. Advancing through thick bush, through the dense rubber and sisal plantations and in the full heat of day, it was impossible for the battalions to advance at the same speed and to maintain contact, so the inevitable straggling occurred and the expected drill movement became an uncontrollable mob.

Superior German fire tactics took their toll and the 63rd Palamcottah Light Infantry ceased to exist as a fighting unit. Its departure forced the attack to move to the right. The 98th Infantry whose morale suffered when the 63rd moved back through them, was being attacked by wild bees which had been roused from their hives in the trees by the high aimed fire.

Some progress into Tanga was made by the two Kashmiri battalions, but on the extreme left the 101st Grenadiers, after putting up a stubborn fight, were forced to pull back. The German counterattack was developing against the British open left flank; Lettow Vorbeck had appreciated that it did not reach further south than the right wing of his own, and as the troops began to withdraw, panic was caused by carriers who, coming under fire, dropped their loads and made for the beaches. They were mistaken for German askaris, and this was the signal for the unreliable regiments to dash for the beaches. Lettow Vorbeck pressed home his counterattack and the British assault crumbled.

Lettow Vorbeck describes the vital phase in the battle: 'The course of the action up till now had shown that the enemy's front, of which the flank was unprotected, did not reach further south than the right wing of our own. Here, therefore, the counterstroke must prove annihilating, and no witness will forget the moment when the

By the end of the battle of Tanga Lettow Vorbeck's askaris had clearly proved their superiority to Major-General Aitken's Expeditionary Force 'B'

machine guns of the 13th Company opened a continuous fire at this point and completely reversed the situation. In the wild disorder, the enemy fled in dense masses, and our machine guns, converging on them from front and flanks, mowed down whole companies to the last man.'

Aitken gave orders to re-embark the next day, 5th November. The movement was covered by the 2nd Loyal North Lancashire and the Kashmir Rifles. Any sound of rifle fire brought panic to the Indian troops and many carriers attempted to swim for the boats. Orders were given that all supplies, ammunition and machine guns were to be left behind. A last appeal by the North Lancs to take the machine guns they were carrying was refused. The order to re-embark was probably necessary, but to leave all the valuable stores and machine guns

Superior German fire tactics took a heavy toll ; the 63rd Palamcottah Light Infantry ceased to exist as a fighting force

behind was senseless and a clear indication of the poor quality of the British commander.

The re-embarkation itself was not without interest, as Meinertzhagen recounts: 'An incident occurred this morning which would have made us laugh if it had not been so pathetic. Our covering party fired a few shots at a German patrol which approached our line and just at that moment when Indian troops were standing on the muddy shore waiting to be taken off in small boats; panic ensued, rifles were thrown away and men rushed into the sea up to their necks, many swimming out towards the transporters. To see whole battalions standing in deep water with only their heads showing, was too dreadful. And the enemy had not fired a single shot! Thank God they never saw it.' So, as Colonel Sheppard had predicted, the Battle of Tanga ended in tragedy for the British.

A study of the results of the first few months of the struggle in East Africa is very important to the under-

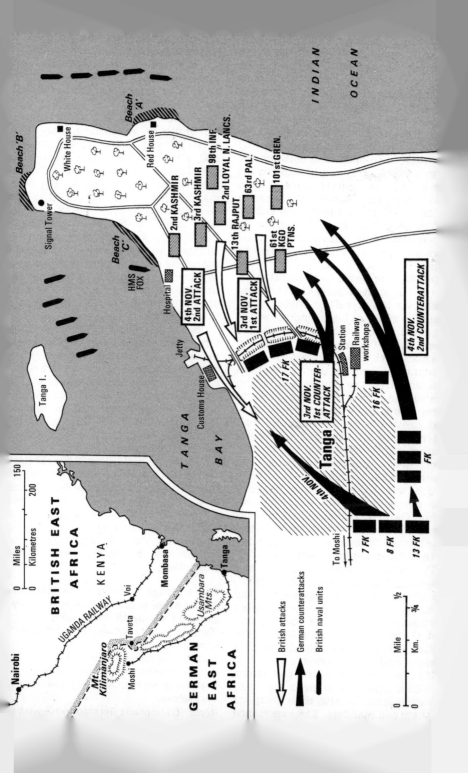

INDIAN OCEAN

Beach 'A'

Beach 'B'

White House

Red House

Signal Tower

Beach 'C'

HMS FOX

Hospital

2nd KASHMIR

3rd KASHMIR

98th INF.

2nd LOYAL N. LANCS.

13th RAJPUT

63rd PAL.

101st GREN.

61st KGO PTNS.

4th NOV. 2nd ATTACK

3rd NOV. 1st ATTACK

Station

Railway workshops

4th NOV. 2nd COUNTERATTACK

Jetty

Customs House

TANGA BAY

Tanga I.

17 FK

3rd NOV. 1st COUNTER-ATTACK

Tanga

4th NOV.

16 FK

FK

7 FK

8 FK

13 FK

To Moshi

Miles 150
Kilometres 200

BRITISH EAST AFRICA

KENYA

Mombasa

Tanga

Nairobi

UGANDA RAILWAY

Voi

Taveta

Usambara Mts.

Mt. Kilimanjaro

Moshi

GERMAN EAST AFRICA

Mile ½ ¾
Km.

British attacks

German counterattacks

British naval units

standing of the conduct of the subsequent campaign, and it is worth summarising the salient factors which contributed to the rout of the British at the Battle of Tanga. In a nutshell, the simple principles of war had been disregarded. The complete lack of surprise, the lack of Intelligence, the failure to make a reconnaissance, and the lack of co-operation between the navy and the army combined with the use of troops of questionable ability, had made the Battle of Tanga a decisive defeat for the British almost before it began. It was to have its repercussions in the fight for East Africa for some considerable time to come.

On 8th November, Expeditionary Force 'B' arrived back in Mombasa, with over 800 casualties, virtually no machine guns and loss of morale which rendered many units unfit to fight for some time. On the other hand, the German victors collected vast amounts of ammunition, as well as clothing, that the British had left on the beaches. They were able to rearm three companies with modern weapons and discard some of their old 1871 rifles. Above all, they had achieved a victory with a loss of only sixty men over vastly superior numbers, and their morale had reached a peak which was to carry them through the remainder of the war when all other German colonies had surrendered. Lettow Vorbeck wrote afterwards that 'Tanga was the birthday of the soldierly spirit in our troops.'

The plan to land at Tanga had originally been conceived in London. No credit had been given to the fighting value of German-commanded African soldiers, nor for that matter had the poor fighting quality of the Indian soldiers been considered. The majority of the regiments used had had little or no training for conditions in which they were to fight and were not even familiar with their weapons or their commanders. The experience of bush warfare in the expeditionary force was nil and yet the offer of a covering force from the experienced KAR had been ignored. British officers still resisted the use of African troops who were really the only soldiers capable of tolerating the severe climatic conditions.

Intelligence, the key to all successful military operations, was non-existent in the British force. The staff had no knowledge of German dispositions or the coastline on which the landing was to take place. The commander had been warned that the Germans, using the railway, could have troops in Tanga within thirty hours, and yet the troops were told not to expect any resistance. In effect, the gathering of Intelligence was regarded by Governor Belfield as necessary only in 'an extreme emergency'. The conduct of a world war did not fall into this category.

Co-operation and concentration of force are two vital requirements necessary for success. The actions of the Royal Navy afford an excellent example of complete disregard of co-operation. The naval commander acted independently and prejudiced the surprise of the landing. He failed to use his naval guns to support the landing and eventually was the first to leave Tanga. The 8,000 British troops with sixteen machine guns, a mountain battery and the 6-inch guns of the *Fox*, were beaten by 1,000 of the German force with only four machine guns and no artillery. The British commander had obviously failed to concentrate his force. The penalty was defeat.

Top: Indian prisoners at Tanga. While the morale of the British force was lastingly damaged, Lettow Vorbeck could say 'Tanga was the birthday of the soldierly spirit in our troops.'
Middle: Captured British officers, ashamed of the poor performance of their force, try to hide their faces from the camera.
Right: Triumphant Germans pose with a captured Union Jack at Tanga. Lettow Vorbeck has won his first major victory

Guerrilla war – 1915 style

It was not surprising that the failure at Tanga prompted the War Office to take control of the operations. The British forces in East Africa were re-organised and two commands were formed, the Mombasa area and Nairobi area, under Brigadier-Generals Tighe and Stewart respectively. The regiments in the two Indian Expeditionary Forces were amalgamated and redistributed between these two commands. Shortly after the reorganisation, Aitken was ordered home in disgrace and command was given to Major-General Wapshare. The disaster at Tanga had been blamed on Aitken; he was not to be employed again and he spent the few remaining years of his life fighting to clear his name.

The Secretary of State for War informed Wapshare that a defensive attitude should be adopted except for minor enterprises, for no further reinforcements could be expected at a time when all available men were required for more vital theatres. In Europe, the Second Battle of Ypres had ended and, with the disastrous experience of Tanga behind them, the British were anxiously conferring with the Belgian authorities as to what action their mutual forces could take

British Service Corps troops provide the logistic backing for the growing Allied forces being sucked into East Africa in pursuit of Lettow Vorbeck's guerrilla columns

37

to contain and harass the Germans in the western areas of German East Africa.

At the outbreak of war, the Belgians had been reluctant to abandon the neutral pose in Africa to which they had agreed in 1885, in spite of the fact that Belgium itself had been invaded by the German army on 4th August 1914. However, the Belgian colonial government was forced to change this posture in the middle of August, for then the neutrality of the Congo was violated when the German gunboat *Hedwig von Wissman* sank some Belgian canoes sailing on the Belgian side of Lake Tanganyika, rendered the Belgian steamer *Alexandre Delcommune* inoperative and landed a party of men commando-style to cut all telephone communications in the area. Such a show of German command of the lake made it impossible for the Belgian government to remain inactive.

At the end of August, the government in Brussels sent instructions to M Tombeur, the then Vice-Governor of Katanga, to expedite the defence of Belgian territory in the Congo, at the same time authorising the Belgian colonial authorities to co-operate whenever and wherever possible with British war proposals in East Africa. It was stressed, however, that their rôle was to be purely defensive, and it was not until a few months later that the plan to conquer Ruanda and the necessity of wresting control of the waters of the lake from the Germans was formulated. Almost within days of the Brussels communication to Tombeur, Anglo-Belgian co-operation was put to the test.

On 5th September, the first German land attack in the area was directed against Abercorn in Rhodesia, but owing to the combined efforts of a small resident force of Northern Rhodesia Police under Lieutenant J J McCarthy and the Mobile Column led by Major H M Stennett, which arrived on 9th September, the attacks were repulsed and the Germans were driven back across the frontier. Meanwhile, assistance had been requested from the Belgian authorities and this duly arrived in Abercorn on 22nd September. Thus a Belgian military contingent now boosted the defenders. As no more attacks seemed imminent, in November the Belgian unit prepared to return to their station in Katanga but were fortunately still available to repel German raiding craft which were harassing settlements along the shores of Lake Tanganyika and attempting to destroy vital telephone and telegraph links in this area.

For the next few months the Belgian force based on Abercorn guarded the southern shores of the lake. The local Rhodesian force became responsible for the defence of the area between Fife and Abercorn. The Belgian military were not too happy with the arrangement. The British insistence that British officers should always be in control of any joint military ventures did not help to smooth the path of Anglo-Belgian understanding and co-operation neither at this time nor later in the campaign. Neither did the confusion in the Belgian mind as to the almost incredible number of commands on the British side help to make such co-operation easier. It is small wonder that in the opening year of the war the Belgians were loath to attack. Nonetheless, after the failure of Tanga, for their part the British were sure that Belgian co-operation was imperative, and with this in view discussions were continued for the next few months both in Elisabethville and London.

Meanwhile, Lettow Vorbeck's overall plan remained unchanged: to attract important Allied troops into East Africa and so divert them from the more vital theatres. However, this far sighted plan was to take some months before its aim was fully achieved. He realised that the British railway was a key factor in the defence of British East Africa and decided that this should become the target. The seizing of the initiative was always his

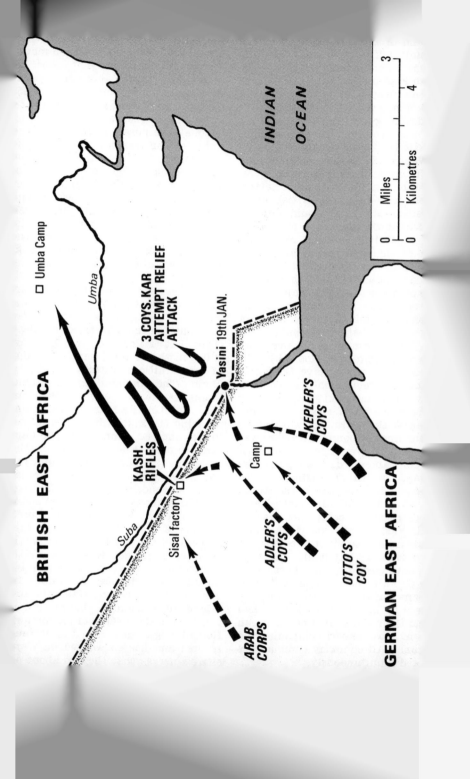

aim, and in this he was aided by the doubtful military quality of the British commanders. One of the British staff officers says of his commander: 'Wapshare is a kindly old gentleman, nervous, physically unfit and devoid of military knowledge; he is much too fond of physical comforts. He is known throughout Kenya as "Wappy". He is a heavy man fond of his food and dislikes exercise.'

At the beginning of 1915 Lettow Vorbeck feared that the British forces in position at Yasini would attempt to push down the coast to Tanga. After a detailed personal reconnaissance of the area, aided by a map prepared by Lieutenant Schaefer, he decided to attack the British position.

The plan was to attack the advanced post of Yasini and encourage the British to commit their reserves on to tactically well-sited German positions. The German companies were ordered up from New Moshi by railway, a factor which gave them tremendous strategic mobility. The efficiency of Lieutenant Kroeber, the officer in charge of the railway, ensured that the operation (working on interior lines of communication) was executed with great speed. A force of nine companies with two guns was assembled south of Yasini by 17th January 1915. The orders for the attack were given on 18th January. Major Kepler with two companies was to attack Yasini from the right flank, Captain Adler also with two companies was to take the left flank. The Arab Corps was posted to the north-west while Captain Otto and the 8th Com-Company advanced frontally, closely followed by Lettow Vorbek's tactical HQ and the main body (one European company, two Askari companies and two guns). All company commanders attacked simultaneously.

A platoon commander in 17 *FK* continues the account: 'We were ordered to join Adler's column and attack the left flank. At 0645 hours I received orders to join in the fight with 1 Platoon. As a rise in the ground on the right hid the enemy from view, the platoon was sent back and moved further round to the left. Here we began at once firing at the enemy who were up in a tower at a range of 150 metres. The platoon gained ground by advancing in rushes, and after fixing bayonets we pursued the enemy who were slowly retreating. The rest of the company in the meantime forced the enemy back to the fortifications of Yasini. We received reinforcement in the shape of one more platoon and two machine guns, but thick bush prevented us from attacking the enemy again. But in spite of this the enemy ceased firing and pulled back. The morale of our men was good and they shot well.'

The Germans then completely surrounded Yasini Camp and the sisal factory. Captain Giffard with three companies of the KAR tried to relieve them but failed, so the Kashmir Rifles in the factory, having run out of ammunition, retired to Umba Camp. The ammunition in Yasini Camp, 300 rounds per man, then ran out. Colonel Rajhbir Singh, commanding the 2nd Kashmir Rifles, was killed, and the command fell to Captain Hanson who, because of the heavy shelling, the lack of ammunition and the exhaustion of the 101st Grenadiers, surrendered. On 19th January the white flag was hoisted over Yasini.

So Lettow Vorbeck had scored another success. The effect of this success on the British, and in particular on their generals, was stultifying and out of all proportion to its military significance. According to one of the British staff officers, 'Sheppard took a most gloomy view of it all and lost all sense of proportion. He had magnified it into a disastrous reverse and has so worked on Wapshare's nerves that they go about as though we had lost the war. It is pathetic seeing two responsible soldiers in such a position. Wappy wanders about murmuring that the War Office will now recall him, while Sheppard considers that his chances

of promotion are ruined by the fall of Yasini. It is disgusting to see all these personal feelings dominating military operations.'

The German victory was attributed to the rapid concentration of the nine companies at a decisive point, good reconnaissance coupled with surprise and a sound tactical plan. While the battle was a victory for Lettow Vorbeck it had a significance for him which was to affect German plans for the rest of the campaign. He commented later, 'Although the attack carried out at Yasini with nine companies had been completely successful, it showed that such heavy losses as we had also suffered could only be borne in exceptional cases. We had to economise our forces in order to last out a long war. Of the regular officers, Major Kepler, Lieutenants Spalding and Gerlich, Kaufmann and Erdmann were killed. Captain von Hammerstein died of his wounds. The loss of these professional soldiers – about one seventh

The German camp at New Moshi, nearly empty because Lettow Vorbeck had moved its garrison by rail in January 1915 to prepare to attack the British advanced post at Yasini

of the regular officers present – could not be replaced.

'The expenditure of 200,000 rounds also proved that with the means at my disposal, I could at the most fight three more actions of this nature. The need to strike great blows only quite exceptionally, and to restrict myself principally to guerrilla warfare was evidently imperative.'

This second British catastrophe resulted in prompt attention from Whitehall. Kitchener despatched a telegram with the following rebuke: 'You are entirely mistaken to suppose that offensive operations are necessary. The experience of Yasini shows you are not well informed of the strength of the enemy . . . you should concentrate your forces and give up risky expeditions in East

Africa where we cannot reinforce you sufficiently to be sure of success.' Would British East African commanders ever learn?

The New Year, then, had started with another reverse for the British forces which weakened further the morale shaken after the defeat at Tanga. Lord Kitchener followed up with a further War Office telegram: 'After careful consideration of the circumstances it is considered that for the present you should adopt a definitely defensive attitude along the Anglo-German frontier from the Lake to the sea . . . Secretary of State desires you to understand that with heavy calls all over the world it is not practicable to meet requirements of East Africa at present.'

The rainy season had started, so the British forces adopted a strategically defensive position. The troops were split into small isolated groups guarding the Uganda railway and the frontier. General Wapshare had no reserve, and because of this tactical imbalance he could no longer counter German moves. The British forces had gone on the defensive tactically as well as strategically, and the initiative was again in the hands of Lettow Vorbeck. The small Indian outposts on the border without British officers neglected the basic infantry task of posting sentries, and they were to prove easy targets for the German askaris.

'Yesterday a bridge at mile 218 on the Uganda railway was blown up by a German patrol. The bridge guard was composed of men of the 98th Infantry. Apparently what happened was this. The men were lounging about without their rifles and were rushed in broad daylight, not a shot being fired in defence. The bridge was then destroyed in a leisurely fashion, rifles removed and the enemy departed, not even taking the trouble to take the men prisoners. Another most disgraceful incident due to rotten soldiering and gutless soldiers. There was not even a sentry on duty and the men merely gaped with astonishment when the

enemy rushed them. What a contempt the Germans must have for our men.

'The written orders given to the sentry at the post were to carry a rifle by night but not by day. This astounding order was signed by the Commanding Officer. The undergrowth was still standing within spitting distance of the bridge and the barbed wire was still a coil, unrolled and thrown into some long grass.' This eye witness account speaks for itself.

In April, Wapshare was ordered to the Persian Gulf and Tighe took over command. His Chief of Intelligence, Meinertzhagen, writing in his diary was frank: 'The chaotic state of affairs here is heartbreaking. No reserve, no discipline, lack of courage in leaders, thousands of unreliable troops and no offensive spirit. I wish to heaven I could get out of it all and fight in the trenches.'

The British, by their defensive attitude and poorly trained troops, had given the German commander the ideal setting for the waging of guerrilla war. As if this were not enough, a further problem now began to rear its head. The health of the British and Indian troops was reaching an all-time

low. This was to be expected in the unhealthy coastal area, but further inland the problem was just as acute.

The Rampur Infantry in April 1915 was reported unfit to march. The 13th Rajput was reported as 'almost incapacitated by sickness'. The MO said 95% needed three month's treatment for malaria. The Allied soldier in East Africa soon had to learn to cope without the usual rations and how to march and keep relatively cheerful on a stomach far from full. He continuously supplemented his meagre allocation of food with fruit he could snatch along the wayside; bananas, pawpaw and mangoes. He sweated under a merciless sun by day and shivered as he slept on the ground by night. Little wonder he could so easily be incapacitated by tropical diseases. Malaria felled senior and junior ranks alike (Smuts was to suffer recurrent attacks for many years after the war); blackwater fever with its exhausting and deadly vomiting was the scourge of the battalions; tick fever stalked the unwary soldier who dropped to sleep on the floor of native huts. The only prophylactic

A German reconaissance plane, one of the reasons for their victory. Yasini taught Lettow Vorbeck to avoid pitched battles, for although he thought that his troops' superiority would ensure victory he was aware that unlike the British he could not afford to sustain high casualties because he had no means of reinforcement from outside the colony

available appeared to be quinine, ordered to be taken by regulations but frequently considered to aggravate rather than prevent the deadly fevers.

The only soldiers in the British force largely unaffected by the harsh conditions were the askaris of the KAR, but because of continued War Office disapproval it took considerable time before more of these excellent soldiers were recruited and trained.

It was no wonder that alarm and despondency were prevalent throughout the British force. Every factor which counts in war appeared to move against them: the trump cards seemed always to be with the Germans. Lettow Vorbeck was now ready to put into practice the lessons he had learnt in SW Africa and to wage one

of the most successful guerrilla wars recorded.

The classic principles of guerrilla warfare – mobility, taking the enemy by surprise, avoiding pitched battles, self discipline, strong command and leadership, and a firm base from which to operate – were factors which were all well understood and applied by the German commander. The Germans were strategically on the defensive, but unlike their adversaries they were tactically on the offensive. The target that Lettow Vorbeck set his forces was the British Uganda railway, the lifeline of the colony which carried all the supplies inland from Mombasa.

A force of company strength was too large to be effective, so it was broken down into small patrols of about ten men, Europeans and askaris, who carried all their supplies and were completely self sufficient. Good training and discipline enabled them to march across miles of waterless, thinly populated desert and blow up the railway and attack the small outposts. As they became more confident and skilful, so their mobility increased and they took the British by surprise, avoided pitched battles and thereby tied down the British force on static guard duties. On their

Above : A raiding party of German mounted infantry. After Yasini guerrilla warfare proper began ; Lettow Vorbeck avoided pitched battles and launched frequent raids on outposts and communications, tying down the British force in static guard duties.
Right : The prime target was the Uganda railway. In two months more than thirty British trains were derailed and ten bridges destroyed

patrols they cut communications raided outposts, captured arms, ammunition and horses.

The stretch of railway between Simba and Samburu came under constant attack. This was getting uncomfortably close to Mombasa. German sabotage was so successful against the line that in two months over thirty trains were derailed and ten bridges destroyed. The British even resorted to the old Boer idea of putting a truck ahead of the locomotive to detonate any charge, but the Germans countered by introducing a delayed explosive charge on the tracks. The new railway which the British were building from Voi was also attacked, and even the area commander, Brigadier-General Malleson, was ambushed while making a

reconnaissance and escaped only because of the gallantry of Sabadai Ghulam Haidar of the 130th Baluchis who covered the retreat of the British car, and for his brave act was recommended for a posthumus VC.

One very successful German patrol captured fifty-seven horses which enabled Lettow Vorbeck to form a second mounted company, thereby giving more mobility and an increased range of patrolling to the German forces.

This episode is vividly described by him: 'One of these patrols had observed near Erok Mountain that the enemy sent his riding horses to water at a certain time. Ten of our horsemen at once started out and, after a two day ride through the desert, camped close to the enemy. Six men went back with the horses: the four others each took a saddle and crept at a distance of a few paces past the enemy's sentries close up to the watering-place, which lay behind the camp. An English soldier was driving the horses when suddenly two men of our patrol confronted him out of the bush and covered him with their rifles, ordered "Hands up". In his surprise he dropped his clay pipe out of his mouth. At once he was asked "Where are the missing four horses?" for our conscientious patrol had noticed that there were only fifty-seven whereas the day before they had counted sixty-one. These four needed light treatment and had been left in camp. The leading horse and a few others were quickly saddled, mounted and off they went at a gallop round the enemy's camp towards the German lines.'

Such brazen and continual raiding parties, the derailing of locomotives, blowing up of railway tracks, and attacking outposts, all had the desired effect of lowering morale among the British troops. This was psychological warfare in its infant stages. The 'Hun' took on the guise of the phantom enemy in the mind of the Allied soldier: in the mind of the British generals the phantom of

Lettow Vorbeck was all too real!

The German commander realised that the war in East Africa was going to be a prolonged one, so preparations were begun to make the colony, and thereby the army, self-sufficient. Even the Governor encouraged the farmers to redouble their efforts to produce more food than ever before, now that it was clear that the German colony was almost completely isolated from any friendly power capable of sending her supplies. Cotton cloth was produced by the ladies of the colony and, with their eyes firmly focused on the war effort, by trial and error they eventually obtained a khaki-coloured dye from the roots of a tree called *Ndaa*. This was especially applauded by Lettow Vorbeck, ever keen to ensure the continued availability of suitably coloured cloth for uniforms for his askaris. Planters rose to the occasion and marketed tyres for bicycles and cars from rubber ingeniously tapped from trees on to rope which was then pressed and shaped to the required thickness. Later, local sulphur, saltpetre and charcoal was used to process the rubber.

A crowning achievement was the production of their own brand of motor fuel. Plenty of soap could be easily supplied by using animal fat or the ever present coconut oil. Tallow and wax were made into candles. From the mangrove swamps on the coast came the tanning materials necessary in the production of vast stocks of boots made near Tanga which were to be invaluable for the *Schutztruppe* operating in the bush in the years to come. The Amani Biological Institute in Usambara began to produce sufficient quinine tablets

The *Schutztruppe* – Intelligence-gathering and card-playing. Intelligence was crucial to this kind of warfare, and although both the British and Germans had an Intelligence system, at first only the Germans paid any attention to their reports

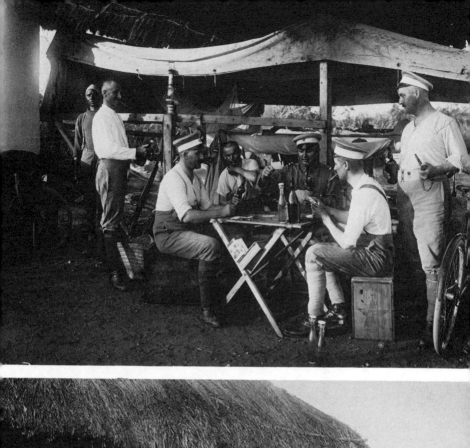

for the entire white settler population in the fight against malaria, the ever present enemy. The efforts of a certain engineer (Herr Rentall) to build a stone bridge over a particularly important river west of Moshi (the Kikafu torrent) to ensure the continued passage of men and supplies in the rainy season was yet another example of the way in which almost every individual in the colony threw himself wholeheartedly into the struggle behind Lettow Vorbeck.

The German force was reorganised and improved. The field and rifle companies became more alike by the cross-posting of Europeans and askaris to even up the balance. The total number of companies was increased to sixty, and by the end of 1915 the strength of the German force was 2,998 Europeans and 11,300 askaris.

To wage this type of warfare successfully, Intelligence is crucial. Both the Germans and the British had an

Above: The King's African Rifles (KAR). In 1915 the KAR was still small, for the British (unlike the Germans) had yet to appreciate that locally recruited Africans would prove to be the best soldiers in this theatre of war. *Right:* The British Carrier Corps, vital in a theatre where the virtual total absence of communications away from the railway required all supplies to be manhandled

Intelligence system, but only the German commanders paid sufficient attention to their Intelligence reports. Meinhertzhagen, the British Intelligence Chief, developed a very sophisticated system and employed many intelligent Swahili-speaking Africans as agents. His own particular brand of Intelligence gathering was called the DPM method (Dirty Paper Method). He found that the German officers' latrines contained much information, if somewhat soiled – old message pads, notes on deciphering codes, private

letters being used as lavatory paper. From this collection of paper he reconstructed all the German officers' signatures and distributed them to all field commanders so that the importance of any captured German document could immediately be recognised and evaluated. Unfortunately Meinhertzhagen's very accurate information was disregarded by the British commanders who did not appreciate that central Intelligence was more accurate than their own locally and haphazardly gathered news, so they refused to take note of the Intelligence reports.

By May 1915 the German commander's overall aim of diverting from other theatres of war to German East Africa as many British forces as possible was rapidly bearing fruit. The 2nd Rhodesia Regiment and a singularly unique regiment, the 25th (Service) Battalion, Royal Fusiliers (Frontiersmen), came to East Africa. The latter was raised and commanded by Colonel Driscoll who had raised and commanded the Driscoll Scouts in the South African War. It included a wealth of fighting experience and individuality. The famous hunter F C Selous was a member, and so was an ex-general from Honduras and many others who had French decorations awarded while serving with the Foreign Legion. In the ranks was a millionaire from Park Lane, a late subaltern from the Garrison Artillery, colour sergeants from the Brigade of Guards, a flunky from Buckingham Palace, a naval wireless operator, cowboys from Texas, Americans from the US Army, in fact a rare assortment of military talent.

The size of the KAR was still only marginally increased, for the report by Colonel Kitchener (brother of Lord Kitchener) had not viewed with favour the arming of so many of the indigenous tribes. It is unquestionable that the African soldier was the best type of soldier for this type of warfare (as the Germans realised), but it was not to be until 1916 that the KAR was

greatly expanded. After surprising difficulty, a Carrier Corps was raised. In a theatre where all supplies had to be manhandled and carried, its formation was vital, its eventual strength rising to 200,000 men.

Tighe, despite close London supervision, considered some offensive action was necessary to restore the morale of the British troops. He decided to attack the German naval base at Bukoba on Lake Victoria. On 20th June the British force (comprising the 2nd Loyal North Lancashire Regiment, the 25th Royal Fusiliers, the 3rd KAR, the 29th Punjabis, one section of the East African Regiment and one section of the 28th Mountain Battery RA) embarked on the ships of the Lake Flotilla and on the night of 22nd June the force moved in on Bukoba.

The Royal Fusiliers landed without opposition and occupied a hill about three miles north of the town, driving off a German piquet of thirty men. The *Rusinga* came up and disembarked the North Lancs and the mountain battery, all of whom were ashore by 1030 hours. The landing party now advanced towards the town and by noon were within a mile of the town. The KAR, landing nearer the town, also took part in the advance.

The progress of the North Lancs was very sticky and slow. They were ordered to turn the German left, but, though their casualties were negligible, they simply would not get on. Meinhertzhagen, who took part in this battle, continues: 'I went over to see for myself what was wrong and found that Jourdain [the CO] was shaking like a blanc-mange, terrified of casualties and thought he had the whole German army opposed to him. I begged him to get on as his turning movement was our main card and if he failed now it would leave us in an awkward position overnight. Nothing would move him, so I told him I would have to recommend Stewart to remove him from command; he fumed and asked me who was commanding the

50

battalion. I told him I would if he would not get on. More fuming, so I sent a helio message to Stewart telling him the Lancs were not being opposed but were anchored owing to the incompetence of their commander. Jourdain then got a peremptory order to advance or hand over to me. He advanced.'

The town was taken by the 25th Royal Fusiliers. The Loyal North Lancashire Regiment worked round it from the north-west with the 3rd KAR in reserve, and Bukoba was entered during the afternoon. The Germans evacuated their positions and pulled back. The British troops proceeded to destroy everything of military value which they could not take away. The Official History well describes the significance of this battle, sometimes referred to as the 'Sack of Bukoba': 'Though not far reaching, the success

General Stewart (in raincoat) at Bukoba on the second day of the successful raid there in June 1915 which did much to restore British morale

of this well-planned operation, gained at slight cost in casualties, did much to restore and revive the morale of the British forces . . . and it made a considerable and valuable impression on the native population.' Seven British troops had been killed: twenty-five were wounded; 32,000 rounds of ammunition and sixty-seven rifles were captured.

During August Tighe pointed out to the War Office, that with the rumoured German replenishment of arms and ammunition coupled with a high sickness rate amongst the British and Indian troops, the military situation in East Africa had become critical.

51

The offensive - Smuts in command

General Tighe's pessimistic forecast for East Africa came at a time when ministers in London were struggling with numerous complex problems in all the principal theatres of war. The Allies were about to launch an offensive in Artois and Champagne on the Western Front, the offensive at Gallipoli had been halted at Suvla Bay and the Austro-German offensive had pushed the Russians back from Warsaw. So it was not surprising that little or no assistance was offered to East Africa from home. But from an unexpected quarter help could possibly now be expected, for by this time the German Protectorate of South West Africa had fallen to Generals Botha and Smuts and the South African forces, and the Union Government was now prepared to send reinforcements to East Africa.

The campaign in East Africa now took on a new complexion, for Colonels Hughes and van Deventer arrived from South Africa to study the means for closer co-operation, and from that moment onwards, South African troops began to arrive. The stimulus of South African support rallied the morale of the settlers and on their own initiative they introduced compulsory service. Not surprisingly, in view of his overall aim in the war, the German commander was delighted

Smuts' troops manhandle a field gun into position

Brigadier-General Northey, commander of the 3,000-strong Nyasaland-Rhodesia Field Force which began moving against Lettow Vorbeck from the south early in 1916

with this news: 'It was important to encourage the enemy in this intention in order that the South Africans should really come and in the greatest strength possible and thus be directed from other more important theatres of war. With greatest energy we continued with enterprise against the Uganda railway.'

The British Prime Minister had directed the Committee of Imperial Defence to consider the problem of East Africa; their findings can be summarised by the following points: steps should be taken to ensure the conquest of German East Africa with as little delay as possible; a new brigade should be sent to East Africa

to bring the total number of white troops up to 12,600; and, finally, co-operation with the Belgians was absolutely necessary.

During November 1915 General Sir Horace Smith-Dorrien was appointed to command the East African forces. His overall plan for the campaign was to engage the German forces in the Kilimanjaro area while a separate force was to land at Dar es Salaam. This was not a new plan, for the foundations had already been laid by General Tighe with the construction of a water pipeline and a railway towards the Kilimanjaro area. The whole scheme was violently opposed by Lord Kitchener, now War Minister; he expressed his fear 'that the proposed reinforcements would prove inadequate,' and that the East African venture was 'a dangerous project in the present state of the war when we require to concentrate all our efforts

Northey's troops bring in German prisoners on the Rhodesian border

on defeating the Germans in Europe'. His objections were over-ruled by the Cabinet but it is well to keep his forecast in mind during the unfolding of the campaign.

Events in the southern area of German East Africa also entered a new phase. Brigadier-General E Northey was appointed as commander of the forces on the Rhodesia-Nyasaland border of the German colony. He arrived in Capetown on 30th December 1915. From this moment on, substantial South African and Rhodesian reinforcements began to arrive. Sir Horace Smith-Dorrien sailed for South Africa at about the same time, but he developed pneumonia during the voyage and had to resign.

The prospect of beginning the offensive made some form of reorganisation necessary. Tighe had concentrated towards the Kilimanjaro area and formed the 1st and 2nd Divisions.

Recruiting in South Africa had gone well and the 1st, 2nd and 3rd South African Mounted Brigades, and the South African Field Artillery (five batteries), were raised.

Further reinforcements came from France, the 40th Pathans and the 129th (DCO) Baluchis, while additional artillery came from Britain together with armoured cars. The Royal Navy Air Service which had taken part in the *Königsberg* operations proved another welcome addition. Its aerial photography was to prove invaluable to the Intelligence effort. The KAR was at last slowly being expanded to 133 officers and 4,200 Africans. General Sheppard had said 'the more African troops we have the better . . . the KAR hardly ever lose a rifle . . . the conclusion every thinking soldier has

Malleson, Tighe and Charlton at
Salaita Hill, scene of the shattering
British defeat at the beginning of the
offensive against the German stronghold
of Kilimanjaro. Tighe's defeat at
Salaita made a lasting impression on
Smuts; henceforward he determined to
outmanoeuvre Lettow Vorbeck rather
than engage him in a stand up fight

arrived at after a year in East Africa
is that only the best and most highly
trained troops can hope to be a match
for the trained African of a fighting
tribe in the bush,' in marked contrast
to his earlier remarks in 1914 about
the mixed bag of troops from India.

The overall size on paper of the
force assembling in East Africa was
impressive. At the end of 1915 there
were 27,350 fighting men, 71 guns and
123 machine guns. The bulk of these
men were British, South African and
Indian units, although more than half
were unacclimatised and inexperienced in bush warfare.

Lieutenant-General Jan Smuts had
been offered the command in November 1915 but had turned it down because of political problems in the
Union. The British government offered
it again on Smith-Dorrien's resig-
nation and this time Smuts accepted.
He was not a soldier by profession but
a lawyer. He had taken office under
Kruger in 1898 as State Attorney of
South Africa; he was then twenty-
eight years old. His military experience was gained during the Anglo-
Boer War 1898–1902 when he was a
daring and successful commander.
Smuts and Botha had concluded with
great success the campaign against
the Germans in South West Africa
which ended in July 1915. There could
have been no better proving ground
for the rigours he was to face in the
East African campaign than these
previous experiences against the
British and Germans.

Smuts reached Nairobi on 22nd
February 1916. Meinhertzhagen records in his diary: 'One cannot talk
to Smuts without being attracted by
his personality. He is a fascinating
little man and one leaves him after an
interview with the impression that he
has a first class brain. I found it such

a pleasure to run over the situation on a map after the laborious processes one had to resort to with Tighe. Smuts grasps points at once and never wants telling a second time.'

Smuts arrived in East Africa just as Tighe's offensive on the German stronghold of Kilimanjaro had begun. It started with a shattering defeat for the British forces at Salaita Hill under Brigadier-General Malleson. This made an impression on Smuts, for during the six months of the South West African campaign only 113 had been killed and 311 wounded, whereas in a few hours fighting at Salaita Hill 133 South Africans were killed.

Meinhertzhagen records: 'Smuts is quite determined to avoid a stand up fight. He told me openly he intends to manoeuvre the enemy out of position and not push them out. He told me he could not afford to go back to South Africa with the nick-name "Butcher" Smuts.'

On arrival in East Africa Smuts, unlike his predecessors, began a very detailed reconnaissance of the German positions, finding out the weak spots of their dispositions. His appreciation of the situation was that an immediate offensive was both necessary and desirable and this view received the blessing of the British government. Smuts decided to adhere to the plan already produced, a converging advance on Kilimanjaro from the north and east, but he decided to move the South African Mounted Brigade from the northern line of advance to the east where it would come directly under his command.

Smuts' plan was that the 1st Division under Major-General J M Stewart was to advance southwards to cut the German lines of communications; it was to move two days before the South African Mounted Brigade in the east. General van Deventer, commanding the South African Infantry and Mounted Brigades, had to seize the Chala Heights as a prelude to executing a turning movement against the stronghold of Taveta. The 2nd

Lieutenant-General Jan Christian Smuts, appointed C-in-C in East Africa early in 1916. A daring and successful commander during the Boer War 1898-1902, he came fresh from more successes against the Germans in South West Africa, July 1915

Division, commanded by Tighe, advancing one day after van Deventer, was to move against Salaita.

On 5th March the 1st Division moved off from Longido but waited until dusk to avoid marching in the heat of the day. Engare Nanuki was reached on 6th March and the division concentrated during 7th March. No opposition had been met. The thick bush in the foothills of Kilimanjaro slowed the division down by another day because Stewart was not prepared to go through thick bush without prior reconnaissance. During this unambitious advance, Smuts was urging speed the whole time, but this had little effect on 1st Division which was held up for a further day by a small German detachment. This sequence of events thereby ensured their

late arrival on the scene of action. The commander had thus failed in his task, for it was not until 14th March that contact was made with the rest of the force.

Meinhertzhagen adds a colourful account in his diary: 'Stewart is still dawdling on the other side of Kilimanjaro and clearly has no intention of even attempting to play the game. Smuts sends him periodical rude messages enjoining haste but the man is quite incapable of making the effort. Smuts is very depressed about Stewart and sees the fruits of his strategy, which has been sound, thrown away.'

In the east van Deventer concentrated the South African Mounted Brigade and Infantry Brigade between the 3rd and 5th March and advanced. By 8th March he had reached the northern wall of the extinct crater in which lay Lake Chala. Lettow Vorbeck says of this advance: 'But it was evident that this enveloping movement of the enemy rendered the Oldorobo position to which we owed many successful engagements during the course of the war, untenable. I therefore decided to deploy the troops for a fresh stand on the mountains which close the gap between the North Pare Mountains and Kilimanjaro to the westward of Taveta.'

Left : General van Deventer, commander of the South African Infantry and Mounted Brigades. Smuts planned to approach Kilimanjaro from the east and north ; van Deventer's task was to seize the Chala Heights and take Taveta from the east. *Top right :* South African artillery at Salaita, part of Tighe's 2nd Division which moved east alongside van Deventer. *Middle right :* KAR mounted infantry move up to Longido prior to advancing on Kilimanjaro from the north. *Bottom right :* The East African Mounted Rifles in action around Kilimanjaro, wearing coloured flashes in their sun helmets to aid recognition in bush fighting

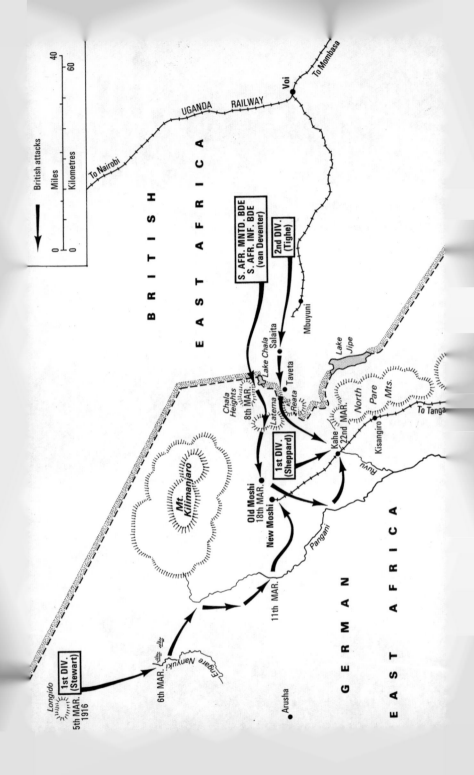

The position on Latema-Reata which Lettow Vorbeck had selected as a defensive position had natural advantages, but he had insufficient troops to cover the hill feature which was some twelve miles in length. It was a difficult time for the Germans, for in front of them they had a vastly superior enemy and the possibility of being cut off (to their rear), but Lettow Vorbeck with confidence says: 'But, in view of the ground, which we knew, and the apparently not too skilful tactical leading on the part of the enemy, I did not think it impossible to give at least one of his detachments a thorough beating.'

Smuts had made a reasonable start, he now had to determine the exact line of retirement of the Germans and discover in what strength the Germans held Latema-Reata. In any event he had to seize this feature before he could advance beyond Taveta.

He decided to attack frontally with the 2nd Division, using the 130th Baluchis, the 2nd Rhodesian Regiment and the 3rd KAR. The attack was very soon held up by effective German fire, the 130th Baluchis and the 3rd KAR suffering the most, losing Lieutenant-Colonel Graham. This was unfortunate for the 3rd KAR, as it was the first time that it had fought as a unit, and it lost more heavily than any other. The loss of Graham was tragic, but it also had three officers killed and about one hundred askaris killed, wounded or missing.

It was decided that a night attack by the 5th and 7th South African Infantry using the bayonet was the best solution. The official despatch clearly indicated the problems: 'This operation was fraught with considerable risk as there was no opportunity of reconnoitring the ground nor was it certain that the enemy was not in large numbers. On the other hand the moon was in the first quarter and so facilitated movement up to midnight.'

The attack was gallantly led by Lieutenant-Colonel the Hon J Byron, whose force reached the ridge but was disorganised on arrival by good mutually-supporting German fire. Some of them held on until daylight, but this fact was unknown to the commander. It was not until daybreak that it was discovered that British troops were on the ridge. Smuts then immediately despatched his reserve, only to find that the German force had slipped away. Lettow Vorbeck had decided to withdraw to Kahe.

Smuts' plan to achieve a decisive victory early on in the campaign had failed; the converging movement from the east had succeeded, but the late arrival of the 1st Division had prevented the plan from succeeding. Smuts should have appreciated that most of 1st Division was inexperienced in this type of warfare and that it would have logistic problems. Nevertheless, the lack of drive and initiative on the part of General Stewart was also a contributory factor in its failure.

The Germans had pulled back in good order and were at liberty to threaten the British lines of communications in the future. Smuts' plan was now to clear the Germans up as far as the River Pangani before the rains started, but prior to the offensive he had decided that there should be changes in the command structure. After a stormy interview, Stewart resigned and left for India; Brigadier-General Malleson, Smuts concluded, had lost the confidence of his men and therefore had to relinquish his command. Also at this time, Tighe left for India, but not in disgrace as did the other two generals. At last there was some firm leadership and direction in East Africa, and promise of a new lease of life seemed to be injected into the campaign.

On 18th March the advance to the Pangani began. Van Deventer was ordered to make a wide flanking movement southwards from Moshi towards Kahe. The 1st Division, now commanded by General Sheppard, was to attack down the road from Moshi while the 2nd Division was to operate from Taveta. The wide flanking movement of van Deventer's forces came up against the River Pangani which proved difficult to cross. The 1st Division bumped well concealed and mutually-supporting German defensive positions. When the attacks went in the Germans had again withdrawn without being brought to battle.

Van Deventer reached Kahe and came under fire from one of the *Konigsberg*'s 4.1-inch guns. Smuts ordered the 1st Division to advance, but it also came under heavy fire from the German positions.

At this point Lettow Vorbeck received reports that the British forces had bypassed Kahe and were threatening his lines of communications. He therefore issued orders for a withdrawal towards Kisangiro and reached the town himself a day later, only to discover that the reports had been false. 'This incident afforded me a remarkable striking proof of the extraordinary difficulties of observing the movements of troops in thick bush and of the great care every commander must exercise in estimating the value of such reports, both of askaris and Europeans in order to base his decision on a foundation that even approximately resembles the reality. In the African bush it is particularly important, whenever possible, to supplement the reports one receives by personal observation.'

On 22nd March, when Sheppard entered Kahe, the town had been abandoned by the Germans and they had left the *Königsberg* gun after first rendering it unserviceable. A chance to destroy the German forces had been lost. With a little more drive it would have been possible to round up the small German force and its commander. The emphasis by Smuts on manoeuvre and outwitting the Germans was good, but it would not bring results unless it was combined with a decisive attack, and the South Africans seemed reluctant to accept casualties.

The action at Kahe brought to an end the first phase of the offensive. Smuts had succeeded in wresting from the Germans the most important part of German East Africa but he had not brought them to battle and inflicted a telling defeat. The British colony was now free from possible attacks and was to serve as the firm base for further penetration into German territory. The vastly different fighting units, British infantry, South African infantry and cavalry, regular Indian regiments, Imperial Service troops from Kashmir, Jind, Kaparthalu, Bhurtpore; the battalions of the KAR, regiments manned by settlers from Rhodesia and Uganda, artillery manned by marines and seamen, were all welded together for the first time into a fighting command. To raise the morale and fighting standards of this widely divergent force to a high level in spite of all the obstacles required a great leader of men. General Smuts had achieved this in a very short space of time.

On the debit side, Lettow Vorbeck, who was awarded the Iron Cross First and Second Class during 1916, had not been brought to battle and defeated by any great tactical victory. Quite the reverse, for he had inflicted considerable casualties on the British forces while executing some brilliant fighting withdrawals. Both his tactical and strategic aims he achieved. He continued to avoid direct confrontation in battle with the Allies which forced the British to send troops they could ill-afford to East Africa rather than employ them where they were even more vitally needed in Europe.

Lettow Vorbeck writes: 'In spite of the various withdrawals we had recently carried out, the spirit of the troops was good, and the askaris were imbued with a justifiable pride in their achievements against an enemy so greatly superior.'

Before continuing with the offensive Smuts decided to reorganise his command, 'not only for the vigorous prosecution of the coming campaign, but also to secure the smooth and

The East African Mounted Rifles camp in the bush before the next advance.

harmonious working of a most heterogeneous army, drawn from almost all continents and speaking a babel of languages.'

Three divisions were formed from the 1st and 2nd Divisions. The 1st Division, commanded by General Hoskins, was to have Indian and British troops, while the 2nd and 3rd Divisions, commanded by Generals van Deventer and Brits, were to receive the South African forces.

A mounted brigade was included with each South African division, 'to secure the necessary mobility to enable us to cope more expeditiously with the enemy askari army of fleet-footed Africans.' This was a strange decision, for already it had been proved that horses were no answer in this type of country: the tsetse fly took far too rapid a toll of them. The campaign in the Cameroons had recently drawn to a close and Nigerian and Gold Coast units would soon become available. The 2nd West Indian Regiment and a battalion of the Gold Coast Regiment were transferred to East Africa.

Another important act was the expansion of the KAR. Training depots were established and askaris were recruited from more numerous tribes. Once trained, they were unrivalled in minor tactics and fire discipline.

Meanwhile, it began to rain. The wet season had arrived. All military operations came to a standstill, roads became impassable, rivers flooded and the plains became lakes. Smuts now planned the next phase of the offensive.

German askaris in action. The German force had been driven from Kilimanjaro but they were retreating in good order. Lettow Vorbeck wrote: 'the askaris were imbued with a justifiable pride in their achievements against an enemy so greatly superior'

820A

Naval operations

The German cruiser SMS *Königsberg* had arrived in East African waters in June 1914. She had been sent to Africa to show the colonists that German naval power could compare with that of Britain. A colonial exhibition was due to open in Dar es Salaam in August and what more glorious a symbol of German power could Dr Schnee, the Governor, invite to impress the Africans than the *Königsberg*?

The presence in East African waters of the German cruiser presented a threat to British shipping and particularly to ships bringing reinforcements from India. The *Königsberg*, armed with ten 4.1-inch guns, was the sister ship of the *Nürnberg* which, as part of Spee's squadron at the Battle of Coronel, had sunk HMS *Monmouth*. She was also faster than any of the three British cruisers of Admiral King-Hall's Cape Squadron (HMS's *Hyacinth*, *Astraea* and *Pegasus*), being capable of a good twenty-four knots. Captain Max Looff, commanding the *Königsberg*, slipped out of Dar es Salaam on 31st July for the open sea and on 6th August proceeded to sink SS *City of Winchester* off Aden. She was not seen again until 20th September when she sailed into Zanzibar and sank the *Pegasus*. The continual patrolling

Lieutenant-Commander G Spicer-Simpson, commander of the British Lake Flotilla, signals from a motor boat on Lake Tanganyika

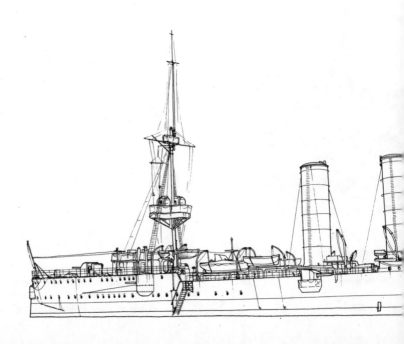

and searching for the *Königsberg* had forced the British ship into Zanzibar harbour for attention to her boilers which were badly furred-up through the use of poor coal. There was nothing to indicate that *Königsberg* was anywhere in the vicinity and consequently, while undergoing repair, *Pegasus* was a ripe sitting target for a surprise attack by the 4.1-inch guns of the *Königsberg* which made short work of her.

Yet another victory was achieved by the German cruiser and a great blow was dealt to British sea power in the Indian Ocean. The effect of these successes was to bring three more

British cruisers into East African waters, the *Chatham*, *Dartmouth* and *Weymouth* under Captain Drury-Lowe, with explicit orders to find and destroy the *Königsberg*.

By this time the German ship was in need of a refit, but to find a concealed harbour along the African coast where contact could be made with German forces was difficult. Eventually Captain Looff decided to bring his large ship up the delta of the Rufiji River, up which she was skilfully manoeuvred as far as her size would allow. Her torpedo tubes were then taken off and stationed at the mouth of the river to tackle any British warships that came near. Her decks were covered with foliage and she became indistinguishable from the surrounding bush. To the British, the elusive *Königsberg* had disappeared again. Nonetheless, they were aware that while the *Königsberg* was afloat no Allied ship in the Indian Ocean was

The German cruiser SMS *Königsberg*. In 1914 and early 1915 she preyed at will on Allied shipping in the Indian Ocean and attracted world-wide attention. By mid-1915 there were six British cruisers looking for her, but she had disappeared

SMS *Königsberg*, light cruiser. *Displacement*: 3,400 tons. *Length*: 378¼ feet. *Beam*: 43¾ feet. *Armament*: Ten 4.1-inch guns and several saluting guns and machine guns, plus two 17.7-inch torpedo tubes. *Armour*: 2-inch deck. *Power/speed*: 3-cylinder triple expansion engines developing 13,200hp and driving two screws/23.5 knots. *Crew*: 350. She was built by the Kiel Dockyard and completed in 1907

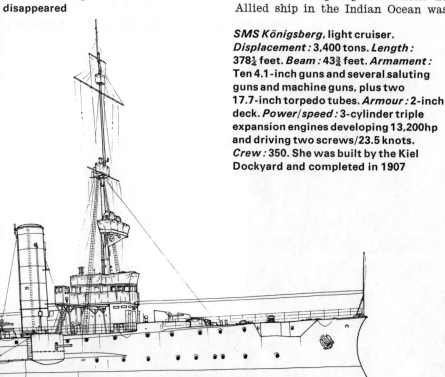

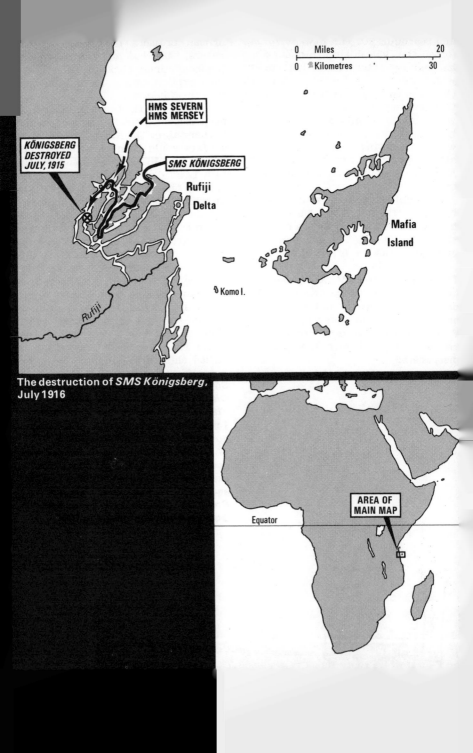

0   Miles   20

0   Kilometres   30

HMS SEVERN
HMS MERSEY

KÖNIGSBERG
DESTROYED
JULY, 1915

SMS KÖNIGSBERG

Rufiji
Delta

Mafia
Island

Komo I.

Rufiji

The destruction of *SMS Königsberg*,
July 1916

Equator

AREA OF
MAIN MAP

safe and no blockade of German East Africa was possible. The hunt for the German ship was intensified.

The first clue as to her whereabouts came with the capture of a German tug by HMS *Dartmouth* and shortly after, the *Chatham* stopped the *President* and took her papers. These papers revealed that coal had been sent from Lindi six miles up the Rufiji. The net was closing in, and on 30th October HMS *Chatham* located the German ship in the delta. The problem now was how to destroy her.

It was learnt from Intelligence sources that the Germans had positioned defences on the banks and entrances of the delta against any seaborne invasion. Brigadier-General Tighe was sent down the coast in HMS *Fox* to investigate the possibility of a combined operation against the German cruiser. But apart from a captured German chart of the river channels, no proper maps were available. 'The grim experience of Tanga only a week earlier was all too vividly in mind.' Nothing was to come of this proposed combined venture.

Air reconnaissance would be the best method of locating the *Königsberg*. In Durban a Mr Cutler owned a 90hp flying boat. He was persuaded to sell his plane to the British Admiralty and accept a commission as a Lieutenant RN. The seaplane was brought up to the island of Mafia near the delta and Lieutenant Cutler located the *Königsberg*'s position. Admiral King-Hall now wanted to know more about the delta, particularly the depth and possible routes up the tortuous river bends. The assistance of a certain Pieter Pretorius was now obtained. Before the war, he had hunted elephant in this part of the German colony and was a well known character in this part of Africa. He set about his daring task with tremendous vigour. His job was to fix the exact location of the ship. From the *Hyacinth*, he was landed at Mafia where he set up base camp. With the assistance of a handful of the locals, Pretorius set out by

canoe in search of the German cruiser.

Scrambling on to dry land, the small party wended its way some miles inland where they came across a wide track, newly cut through the *pori*. Further discreet observation revealed lines of Africans guarded by German soldiers carrying what appeared to the watching band to be supplies. During a lull in the operations, two of the porters were ambushed and persuaded to confirm the suspicions of the search party that indeed it was the *Königsberg* moored some way off. Further persuasion resulted in Pretorius being guided by the prisoners to within 300 yards of the cruiser.

Her exact location plotted, as furtively as he had arrived Pretorius and his men slid out of the coastal swamp back to the small island of Komo. A second reconnaissance was ordered by Admiral King-Hall to find and plot the position of the torpedoes. This he achieved in collusion with a local chief and his own disguise as an Arab trader.

His most difficult task was to find out which of the numerous channels of the Rufiji were navigable, for not until he had all this information was King-Hall prepared to strike. The *Königsberg* had held the Royal Navy up to ridicule on the high seas; the admiral was not prepared to hazard a failure.

The dauntless Pretorius and his band spent night after night sounding the depths of the delta with a long pole. The possibility that a channel had been mined was but one more risk this daring man took. But at the end of it all, he established the fact that shallow-draughted monitors should be able to negotiate a passage close enough for their 6-inch guns to get within sight of the German cruiser. (The original plan that two seaplanes should bomb the immobilised cruiser was abandoned when one of the planes crashed into the sea and was a write-off.)

Two monitors, meanwhile, the *Severn* and the *Mersey*, were making slow progress from Malta through the Red Sea. They finally arrived off the

Rufiji at the beginning of June. It was not until the first week in July 1915 that Admiral King-Hall at last decided that the time was ripe to attack the *Königsberg*. Using a chart compiled by Pretorius, the *Severn* and the *Mersey* sailed up the north channel of the delta. Guided by a seaplane, and in spite of German gunfire from the jungle-covered banks, they sailed relentlessly towards their objective. However, it appeared that Captain Looff had half-expected such an attack. The guns of the cruiser fired at the small vessels and their aim was accurate enough to force both her attackers to fall back and retire. But King-Hall could not give up now.

Five days later, the *Severn* and the *Mersey* returned to the fray and this time they were successful. Again directed on to their target by a seaplane, their guns found the correct range. Outnumbered, the *Königsberg* was soon a blazing furnace, and as a fighting ship she was destroyed beyond repair.

But it was not to be the end of the *Königsberg*, for her 4.1-inch guns were salvaged by the Germans and the

Above: The British Monitor *HMS Severn* moves up the Rufiji Delta, eventually located as the *Königsberg*'s hiding place. *Right:* Rifle and machine gun fire, directed at the *Severn* and her sister ship the *Mersey* from the jungle-covered banks of Rufiji. At their first attempt the Monitors were driven back by the *Königsberg*'s guns

ghost of the *Königsberg* turned up again and again in the shape of her guns during the land campaign. They were bigger than anything the British had and were to prove very effective on numerous occasions. The cruiser itself lay useless and battered in the Rufiji delta for the remainder of the war, and is still there to this day.

The inland frontiers of German East Africa were bounded in part by three great African lakes, Victoria, Tanganyika and Nyasa. Lake Tanganyika formed a vast inland sea some 400 miles long and fifty miles wide at its narrowest point. Its strategic importance lay in the fact that down its centre from north to south ran the boundary between German East Africa and the Belgian Congo. Such a long

The wreck of the *Königsberg*

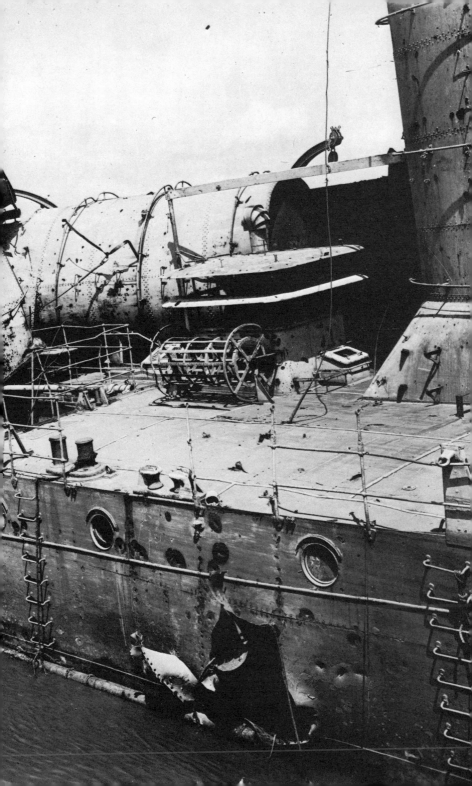

Top left : Left to rot, the wreck
of the *Königsberg* (with the graves of
her fallen sailors), destroyed by the
Severn and *Mersey* at their second
attempt five days later. The wreck is
there to this day. *Left :* The ghost of the
Königsberg in action – her crew
salvaged her 4.1-inch guns and they saw
action again and again in the land
campaign. *Above :* A Royal Naval party
goes up-river to inspect the destroyed
Königsberg

stretch of water naturally facilitated
troop movement from north to south.
At the beginning of the war, Lettow
Vorbeck with the assistance of three
gunboats on the lake had effectively
exercised undisputed control in the
area. He had formed a marine detachment of about 400 rifles. His fleet consisted of the *Hedwig von Wissman*, the
Graf von Gotson and the *Kingani*, all
armed with 3.5-inch naval guns.

This undisputed control of the lake
by the Germans attracted the attention of Mr John R Lee, a big-game
hunter. He felt that German control
in the area could be broken. In April
1915, while in London, he approached
the Admiralty and suggested that a
naval detachment, plus boat, should
be brought overland from South Africa
to the lake. Remembering their reception of more mundane requests in
regard to movements in East Africa

earlier in the war, it might be thought
that such a fantastic suggestion
would be filed away in the recesses of
the Admiralty. Almost unbelievably,
this was not to be the case. Either Mr
Lee himself must have been an over-
whelmingly convincing character to
impress such a daring scheme on the
First Sea Lord, Sir Henry Jackson, or
the latter was prepared to grasp at
any straw, however frail, to attempt to
restore British naval pre-eminence in
waters where this was undoubtedly
being rapidly undermined by growing
German naval activity. So it was that
one of the more fascinating, if a trifle
comic, episodes of the First World War
began. Sir Henry not only supported
the Lee idea, he went further and
suggested that two boats be sent
instead of one.

Command of this expedition was
given to Lieutenant-Commander G
Spicer-Simson. Very quickly he was
selecting and briefing his team in
London. 'We're going to take out two
motor-boats with guns and stores to
Capetown by sea, thence by rail to
Elisabethville, but soon after that the
railway line comes to an end and
there's a rather difficult stretch of
more or less virgin bush to be surmounted, about 150 miles.'

This was to be no ordinary naval
expedition. Two boats were found in
Messrs Thornycroft's yard at Twicken-

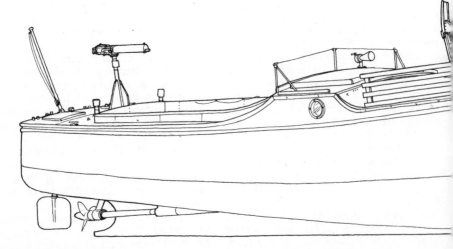

The gunboats *Mimi* (foreground) and *Toutou* on trials on the Thames. Their mission, which began when they left England in June 1915, was to destroy the German gunboats which dominated Lake Tanganyika and were seriously delaying Allied operations in East Africa

ham on the Thames, forty feet long, eight foot beam, with two 100hp petrol engines giving a speed of nineteen knots. They had no names and Spicer came up with the idea of *Cat* and *Dog*. The Admiralty disliked this and instead *Mimi* and *Toutou* were selected! The next thing was their armament, and 3-pounders were selected for the bows with Maxims aft.

The party of two boats, four officers and twenty-four seamen set sail from Tilbury in the *Llanstephan Castle*, reaching Capetown on 2nd July. The boats were moved by rail from Capetown to Fungurume which was reached on 5th August. But it was not until 15th August that the traction

engines arrived to pull them on the next part of their journey to Sankisia. the ensuing part of the road journey took six weeks and proved to be the most arduous, a battle against the African heat, lack of water and mountain ranges. At Sankisia the boats were loaded onto the railway again and thence to Bukama where they were launched on the River Lualaba. The river at this time of year was shallow, so teams of native paddlers were hired and the boats taken up the river in this manner to prevent damage. On arrival at Kabale, *Mimi* and *Toutou* were put on the railway again, reaching Lukuga on Lake Tanganyika on 28th October, the end of a fantastic journey and the beginning of an even more incredible naval action.

On 26th December the German ship *Kingani* was sighted. It was a Sunday. Spicer finished the church service and then ordered immediate action. Both *Mimi* and *Toutou* chased the German

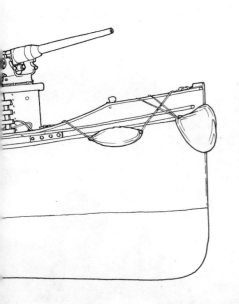

Specially adapted for operations on Lake Tanganyika were two motorboats, nicknamed *Mimi* and *Toutou*. These each had a length of 40 feet, a beam of 8 feet, a top speed of 15 knots and armament comprising one 3-pounder (which could be fired only dead ahead, as the structure of the foredeck on which the gun was mounted was not stressed to withstand a lateral recoil, which would tear the gun from its mounting) and a Maxim machine gun in the stern

Top left : A traction engine pulls *Mimi* and *Toutou* over one of the 200 bridges specially built during the 2,800 mile overland journey from Capetown to Lake Tanganyika. *Left : Mimi* is loaded onto the railway at Sankisia. *Bottom left :* The two gunboats on the River Lualaba at Bukama. *Above :* Preparing to attack the *Kingani*, one of the three German gunboats dominating Lake Tanganyika. After this successful action on 26th December 1915 the *Kingani* was repaired, re-equipped and renamed the *Fifi*

vessel. Coming in to closer range, they opened fire and very soon the Germans hoisted their white flag of surrender. The German ship was pulled ashore, repaired and given two guns, and Spicer then renamed her HMS *Fifi*.

The Admiralty read Spicer's report on the victory with much satisfaction, and promoted him to commander. A special parade was held and a telegram from England read out, 'His Majesty's congratulations to his most remote expedition.' Morale in Spicer's command was high. It was not long before another engagement was imminent, for on 9th February the *Hedwig von Wissmann* was sighted. Spicer ordered *Fifi* and *Mimi* to sea, and they both closed in on the German ship. In a very short time the *Hedwig* was ablaze and sinking from the bows; her stern rose out of the water and she went down.

The *Graf von Gotson* was seen on the following day, but Commander Spicer-Simson refused to put any of his boats into action and the German ship steamed out of sight. It was possible that he feared his luck would run out or that he was the type of person who could not accept a failure. Whatever the reason, because of his action morale suffered badly and his prestige with the men sunk very low.

Soon after this refusal, General Northey ordered Spicer-Simson to move down towards Bismarckburg to support an attack on the fort. The little fleet duly arrived and they observed three *dhows* used for carrying German troops. Spicer-Simson's officers urged him to attack. He refused, stating that it would bring his boats within range of the guns of the fort. So the German *dhows* were allowed to escape. On landing Spicer-Simson learned from Colonel Murray that the *dhows* contained escaping German askaris. Yet again he had failed. He believed that his two victories would make his name in naval history and he was not prepared to risk that, even at the price of being branded a coward.

The story of the Lake Tanganyika Flotilla came to an end. The crews had surmounted incredible obstacles in actually getting their boats to the lake and they had achieved two decisive victories. The sinking of the *Hedwig von Wissmann* had made possible the long awaited co-operation between the Belgian and British forces. Now the former agreed to attack from the west and north-west, and the advance towards the German capital of Tabora began. This colourful little expedition had in fact played a significant part in the campaign in German East Africa in spite of its unstable commander.

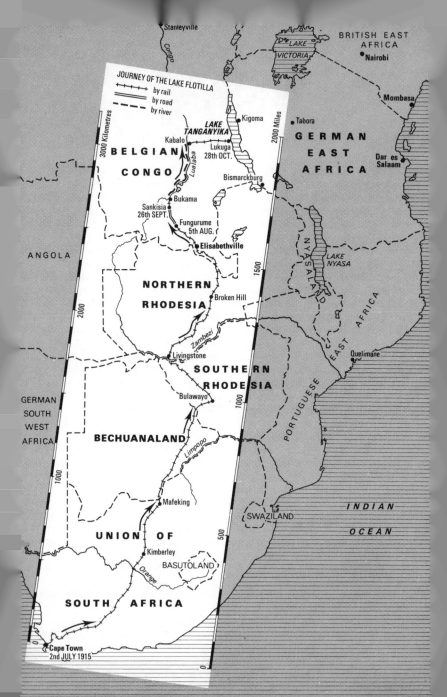

JOURNEY OF THE LAKE FLOTILLA
++++++ by rail
────── by road
‒ ‒ ‒ ‒ by river

STANLEYVILLE

Congo

LAKE VICTORIA

BRITISH EAST AFRICA

Nairobi

Mombasa

Kigoma

LAKE TANGANYIKA

Tabora

GERMAN EAST AFRICA

Dar es Salaam

Kabalo

Lukuga 28th OCT.

BELGIAN CONGO

Lualaba

Bismarckburg

Bukama

Sankisia 26th SEPT.

Fungurume 5th AUG.

Elisabethville

NYASALAND

LAKE NYASA

ANGOLA

NORTHERN RHODESIA

Broken Hill

Zambezi

Livingstone

PORTUGUESE EAST AFRICA

Quelimane

SOUTHERN RHODESIA

Bulawayo

GERMAN SOUTH WEST AFRICA

BECHUANALAND

Limpopo

Mafeking

SWAZILAND

INDIAN OCEAN

UNION OF SOUTH AFRICA

Kimberley

BASUTOLAND

Orange

SOUTH AFRICA

Cape Town 2nd JULY 1915

Journey of the Lake Flotilla, from 2nd July to 28th October 1915

Above : Prisoners from the *Hedwig von Wissmann*, the second of the German gunboats to be attacked. She was sunk, burning furiously, on 9th February 1916
Below : The wives of a local chief celebrate the sinking of the *Hedwig von Wissmann*. By the end of February the British Lake Flotilla had swept Lake Tanganyika clear of German craft and the Allied offensive could begin

The Allies close in

By 1st April 1916 Smuts had reorganised the British force into three divisions, and had established his GHQ at Old Moshi, 4,800 feet above sea level. With a guaranteed superiority of numbers, he began to plan the next phase of the campaign.

The conquest of the Kilimanjaro and Arusha area close to the borders of the British Protectorate was the obvious initial move. It was from this area that the German patrols ventured forth against the British life line, the Uganda/Kenya railway; it was also in this area that the German colonists had concentrated their developments.

The next phase was not so simple. German East Africa was a vast territory with poor roads and no major towns. On the other hand the two railways were of immense strategical importance, as had been shown in the Battle of Tanga in 1914. So was the Tabora area which produced many German askaris. All available Intelligence indicated that the Germans intended to offer resistance for as long as possible in the Pare and Usambara Mountains and then fall back on their main recruiting area, Tabora. Smuts concluded that a faulty initial strategy 'might lead to months of futile marching and wasted effort', but his staff were not quite so sure that he had considered the factors dispassionately in his assessment.

The *Schutztruppe* man a machine gun against a British reconaissance plane

Colonel Meinertzhagen put it well in his diary: 'Smuts is irresistibly drawn towards Lettow Vorbeck and if he persists he will lose the initiative and the campaign will end in simply following Lettow Vorbeck about wherever he chooses to wander. He is more mobile than we are and is operating in his own country. But we have vastly superior forces and should force the pace and dictate operations, making him fight us where we will and not where he wishes.'

The first course open to Smuts was to advance inland by attacking Tanga and Dar es Salaam. This was rejected even though this policy had been a success in German South West Africa; possibly the memory of the Battle of Tanga still lurked in the commander's thoughts. The difficulty of landing a large army at Dar es Salaam with its narrow dangerous harbour entrance during the monsoon season could easily prove an impossible task, and the coastal area after the rains would also present a severe health risk. Smuts was wise to reject this course of action. The second possibility was to move south from Lake Victoria via Mwanza against Tabora. This would mean long exposed lines of communications, but it would also be a direct threat to the Germans' best recruiting areas. The main objection to this course of action was that it engaged the Germans in one area only. Smuts commented, 'to occupy so huge a territory as German East Africa within a reasonable time, a simultaneous advance from different points along different routes was essential.'

The final course open was to attack southwards from Kilimanjaro with a two-pronged assault, one directed along the Usambara railway, the other towards the central railway via Kondoa Irangi. Meanwhile, simultaneous attacks would be made by the Belgians in the west and General Northey in the south. This was the plan that Smuts adopted. It suffered from the obvious military failing of lack of concentration, but far more important was the fact that the Germans expected the advance to come along the Usambara railway and they had concentrated their forces there to meet such an attack. Apart from the odd German company in the centre of German East Africa, the colony was left unguarded Smuts had been given faulty information by local Afrikaner settlers who stated that military operations would come to a standstill because of the rains. In his despatch to Whitehall, Smuts made no mention of where his decisive action would take place. The aim should have been to hit the Germans in a decisive encounter. Meinertzhagen stated: 'What we want to get at is the enemy's main force. Strategic points are useless except with that object in view. For that reason a single man more than the minimum on the Usambara railway is a waste of force.'

Nevertheless, Smuts considered that it was essential to attack the German colony from other directions. Brigadier-General Sir Charles Crewe was despatched to link up with the Belgians under Tombeur. His task was to see that a maximum degree of co-operation existed with the Belgian force in their planned attack from the west. Northey's force on the Nyasaland border was also to be co-ordinated into the overall plan envisaged by Smuts, and reinforced.

The plan which was finally decided upon can best be summarised in Smuts' own words: 'Merely to follow the enemy in his very mobile retreat might prove an endless game, with the additional danger that the enemy forces might split up into guerrilla bands doubling back in all directions and rendering effective occupation of of the country impossible. In view of

Top : A supply train on the Uganda railway, the British lifeline in the Kilimanjaro area. *Right :* Sabotaged by German raiders. In April 1916 Smuts began to plan the next phase of the campaign, the push south from Kilimanjaro

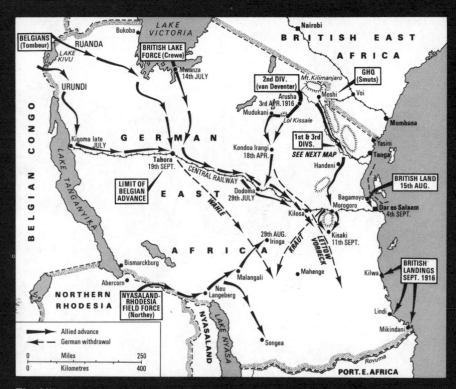

The Allies close in, 1916

the size of the country it was necessary to invade it from various points . . . General Northey was operating eastwards from Lake Nyasa: a Belgian column was launched eastward from north of Lake Tanganyika, a mounted brigade under van Deventer was launched towards Kondoa Irangi and finally three columns advanced southeast against the Usambara Mountains.'

During the last week of March, van Deventer, commanding the South African Mounted Brigade, concentrated on Arusha and on 3rd April he started his dash for Kondoa Irangi which was to become one of the outstanding cavalry feats of the First World War. The remainder of the 2nd Division, the 3rd South African Infantry Brigade commanded by General Berrange, followed at their best infantry speed.

Misguidedly, the South Africans had listened to the advice of local Afrikaner settlers that the brunt of the rainy season would fall on the Kilimanjaro regions, and that farther south and west the weather would not hold up any campaigning. The way to Kondoa and the central railway would be open.

But how wrong the local farmers were! The rains came down across the open grasslands, and at every occasional thicket a German patrol was waiting to attack and ambush the flagging horses. The Mounted Brigade pushed rapidly forward and located the first German position on the hill of Lolkisale, the only source of water for miles. The South Africans, using the traditional Boer tactics of working uphill from boulder to boulder and firing at each puff of smoke, gained ground and seized the hill, but the real enemy was the severe thirst that both men and horses were beginning to suffer, rather than the German askaris. The feature of Lolkisale was seized and the way to Kondoa Irangi was now clear for van Deventer's 2nd Division.

At this point van Deventer despatched a squadron of the SA Horse on a flank-protecting mission to Mudu-

Brigadier-General Sir Charles Crewe, commander of the British Lake Force which seized Mwanza on Lake Victoria in July, and then moved south to join with the Belgian force advancing east from Lake Tanganyika

kani. But the cavalry had not been forewarned that this was a tsetse-infested area: they appreciated this only as their soaking and bedraggled mounts began to wane and die. Within a week, one fifth of them had been left by the wayside. The remainder of the SA Mounted Brigade moved forward in spite of the heavy loss of horses, while the infantry toiled along behind through the mud and rain. The rains, which had come late this year, were to affect the conduct of this campaign considerably. The tragic loss of animals was important, for up to this point 250 horses and sixty mules had died. Resupply became almost impossible; lorries became bogged down, needing teams of mules to pull them out of the mud. The wireless had broken down, motor cycles could not get through the mud and the only means of communications were mounted orderlies posted at intervals of ten miles.

The gallant SA Mounted Brigade, now (12th April) only 880-strong and having lost a further 140 horses and fifty mules, pushed on through impossible conditions and on 18th April attacked Kondoa Irangi. The force at this stage had become unbalanced, for the infantry were well behind and it must be appreciated that single arms working on their own cannot achieve decisive results. It is only by the close co-operation of cavalry, infantry and artillery that victory can be achieved. On 16th April the cavalry were within seven miles of Kondoa Irangi, their strength at this time being 650 men, and more horses had been lost.

Robert Dolbey, a medical officer with the 2nd Division, recounts: 'Lying beside the road with outstretched neck and a spume of white froth on nose and muzzle, are the horses of the 2nd Mounted Brigade; with bodies swollen by the decomposition that sets in so rapidly in this sun and smelling so high heaven, are the fine young horses that came so gallantly through Kahe some ten days ago. Brits violets the tommies call them as they seek a site to windward to pitch their tents. For this is horse sickness, the plague that strikes an apparently healthy horse dead in his tracks.'

The SA Mounted Brigade seized Kondoa Irangi, and the Germans withdrew in good order, destroying what they could not take with them. While the German forces retreated, the 1st SA Brigade had achieved its mission in record time, but with its strength now less than 600 it was completely immobilised.

Meinertzhagen commented: 'Our capture of Kondoa Irangi took the enemy by surprise. They never suspected we could move so quickly over bad roads in the rains. Neither did they credit Smuts with so bold a move. I doubt whether any British general with British troops could have planned and carried out the move in tropical Africa in the rains. Only South Africans born and bred to long distances and living on the country could have accomplished it.'

The infantry took more than a fortnight to catch up with the mounted troops, suffering considerable losses, not from German action but rather from disease and exhaustion. Kondoa Irangi was situated on an easily defensible position. The town itself was in a valley surrounded by small hills, and it was there that defensive positions were eventually built, the South Africans having a distinct reluctance to dig trenches. Lettow Vorbeck transferred a number of companies to the area to hold the British advance, and the Usambara area was thinned out. Meinertzhagen, in his Intelligence appreciation for GHQ, realised this had been done, but his assessment was not accepted until too late. The German plan was clear to him: they were prepared to abandon the Usambara railway as soon as the British moved south from Moshi. He felt that Lettow Vorbeck had concentrated the bulk of his forces near Dodoma and was preparing to attack van Deventer. It is interesting to get van Deventer's views: Meinertzhagen asked him: ' "Are you well dug in" – no reply. "For God's sake do not despise the enemy" I said.

"Damned Kaffirs" says he, and then adds to Nussey [GSO1 2nd Division] "Are we dug in?"

'Nussey smiles at me and van Deventer comes near to a smile. Nussey was at Spion Kop, van Deventer at Tugela Heights. If they had been at Paardeberg they would have more faith in trenches.'

Meinertzhagen continued: 'Van Deventer is calm and collected, divulging his plans to none, not even his staff. He is as cunning as an old fox and does not make up his mind until the last moment and then he acts like lightning; up to that moment he appears dense and slow. To him a decision is final; there is no swerving, no delay, no alternative plan. At moments he can be acutely acid. He experiences some difficulty in not realising he is the hunter and not the hunted, for during the Boer War he was accustomed to the latter role.'

As was expected, on 9th May Lettow

Vorbeck attacked with 9, 14 and 24 *FK* (Captain Otto), 15 and 19 *FK* (Colonel von Bock), and 18, 22 and 27 *FK* (Captain von Kernatzki), in all some 4,000 men. It was now clear that Lettow Vorbeck had reinforced this area and obviously the Usambara front was weaker, as Meinertzhagen had assessed.

An eye witness of the battle at Kondoa Irangi continues with the account:

'At 4pm the camp was awakened by the bursting of a shell from a large gun. The projectile exploded quite close to us and shook the house. But the gun was an enemy mistake, for it warned us. We were sitting having supper when quite suddenly the loud rattle of musketry electrified us. The whole camp blazed and we could see the pitiful little flashes of rifles and hear the cheering of troops on the ridge. Night work has always fascinated me so I rushed out and made my way towards the firing. Rifle and machine gun fire were deafening as I approached camp ridge. Two determined assaults were driven back, the second with a bayonet. By 10 am the crisis approached, I advised

A mule is brought across a rainswollen river by cable. The conduct of the campaign in 1916 was considerably affected by the coming of the rains which caused the virtual breakdown of the logistic system

Calendar to counterattack. He wouldn't but the South African soldiers behaved splendidly, quite steady, quiet and collected. Their fire discipline was perfect. The troops are fine material. They are more mobile, self reliant and better able to live on the country than British troops.'

The German attacks failed to achieve any objective, but Lettow Vorbeck got very close to giving van Deventer a lesson. Both sides now contented themselves with holding a defensive position and patrolling activity. The mobility of the 2nd Division was by now very limited, for horses were still dying and no remounts were available. But more Afrikaner reinforcements were beginning to come forward to van Deventer's command.

A new reserve was formed after the arrival of the 7th, 8th and 10th SA Infantry, 28th Mountain Battery and a host of other minor units, including the South African Motor Cyclist Corps, the Volunteer Machine Gun Company and the 10th Heavy Battery which was using the guns of the sunken *Pegasus*.

The incredible dash to Kondoa Irangi by the South African Mounted Brigade, while spectacular, did not achieve the strategic significance that would have been possible if there had been a correct balance of forces. It was not until mid-July that the 2nd Division, after reinforcement, was again capable of movement. The advance to Kondoa Irangi had not been exploited and the fruits of this notable cavalry achievement were lost. It is interesting to speculate what the results would have been had Smuts placed another division in reserve and made more logistic support available to van Deventer to make exploitation possible.

By the middle of May the rains had slackened in what was one of the heaviest rainy seasons on record. Smuts was now resolved to move at the earliest possible moment and clear the Germans from the Pare and Usambara Ranges.

Major Kraut, who commanded the German Usambara forces, had despatched part of his force to Lettow Vorbeck in Kondoa Irangi to halt 2nd Division's advance, and he was now reduced to about 2,000 rifles. Smuts decided the time was now ripe to push down the Usambara railway. He reorganised the 1st and 3rd Divisions into three columns. Brigadier-General Sheppard commanded the river column which was to move down the bank of the River Pangani. The centre column, commanded by Brigadier-General Hannyington, was to clear the railway, and Colonel Fitzgerald of the KAR was to push along the eastern edge of the mountains. The divisional reserve was commanded by General Hoskins, and Smuts himself commanded the force reserve.

The Usambara Mountains were high and virtually impassable: on their eastern side were fertile valleys, but the western slopes fell steeply to the railway and main road. The River Pangani, wide, rapid and unfordable, flowed on this side.

The three Allied columns advanced without encountering much opposition, but the conditions were appalling. Sickness was taking a great toll of the men, and the troops had been on half rations, the logistic backing having virtually broken down. Furthermore the division might well have run out of ammunition had heavy fighting been encountered. Major Kraut withdrew his German forces to Buiko to avoid being cut off by a greatly superior force.

Smuts halted at Buiko on 31st May: 'the rapidity of the advance had exceeded my best expectations. We had reached the Usambara in ten days, covering a distance of about 130 miles over trackless country.' But at this point the force had outstripped its logistic backing and a pause was necessary to bring up supplies and repair the railway and roads. To maintain this large army composed of many races with differing requirements put a heavy burden on the administrative resources.

The strain on the administrative backing was to become greater as the campaign increased. During their withdrawal, the Germans had successfully destroyed the railway, thus making the task of the 25th, 26th, and 28th Sappers and Miners very difficult. They were indeed some of the hardest working troops in Smuts' command. Throughout the campaign, the railway was carrying repair material and the requirements of the army. It is important to note that relaying and repairs on the railway were carried out at one to two miles per day, a speed that was seldom exceeded during peace. Never was the campaign delayed through the failure of the railway to bring up reinforcements or supplies.

The halt at Buiko lasted four days.

Ruwu bridge, a suspension bridge repaired by Indian Sappers after the Germans had destroyed it

Smuts now visited 2nd Division at Kondoa Irangi to discuss his plan with van Deventer. His aim was to gain Handeni, thereby driving a wedge between Lettow Vorbeck and Kraut. A dual advance to the central railway might then trap the German forces and so bring Lettow Vorbeck to a decisive battle.

Smuts decided to advance to Handeni with the overall aim of occupying the central railway at Morogoro and Dodoma. The move towards Korogwe went reasonably well apart from the difficult conditions and a few small dug-in German positions. Korogwe was seized after a fine attack on Zuganatto bridge by the 3rd KAR. Smuts had said that the KAR could march faster than the South African Cavalry. He had already ordered the raising of more KAR units, so that the strength by June was doubled to 380 officers and 8,100 men.

The Official History recognises the African soldiers' ability. 'This success on which 3rd KAR was warmly congratulated was a good example of the speed and skill with which, under resolute leadership, the African troops

were able to work in the bush by night.'

The German withdrawal proceeded unhindered and Smuts entered Handeni on 18th June. Meinertzhagen comments: 'It is remarkable that on no single occasion have we won a fight and been able to reap the whole fruits of victory. The enemy always manages to slip away. The reason is not far to seek. Over-cautiousness and failure to develop a real flank attack. On no single occasion has any effort been made to get astride the enemy's line of communication.'

The advance towards Morogoro continued while air reports had confirmed that Kraut had prepared defensive positions on the River Lukigura near Makinda. Smuts had now decided to form a flying column comprising the 25th Royal Fusiliers, the 2nd Kashmir Rifles and the 5th and 6th SA Infantry. It is interesting to note that because of sickness these regiments were down to 170-200 men each. The

The British push south towards Morogoro, squeezing Lettow Vorbeck into the south-eastern corner of German East Africa

plan was that Sheppard's column was to pin the Germans down frontally and the flying column to make a flanking move. This was achieved. The Germans were pinned down frontally mainly by the armoured cars in his force, and the flying column got under way with a flanking move. The 25th Royal Fusiliers are interesting to follow in this action for they were typical of the troops in Smuts' force. An officer of that regiment, writing soon after the event, says 'I have never seen men more utterly tired and woebegone than our men; they had been marching twenty-four and a half hours, kit-laden and without substantial food, and yet when they went into battle all fatigue was forgotten, they were careless of further physical trial.'

The flying column pushed home the attack and tackled the German positions with the bayonet, a rare occurrence in this campaign. The battle turned out to be a great success, and this action, although small, was the most notable success achieved by the 1st Division and proved that the out-flanking move so often attempted could succeed.

The morale of the force went up and their confidence in the commander was enhanced, but the force was halted through sheer attrition. In just over one month, Smuts' columns had marched over 200 miles and the army needed a halt, 'the absence of such minor luxuries as soap, cleaning materials and tobacco, and of all recreation for troops off duty, tended further to depress the exhausted and hungry men.'

The difficulties of evacuating the sick and bringing up food supplies are best described by a medical officer: 'The numerical strength of the forces defeated its own object, establishing a vicious circle. It was impossible to feed the large number of troops so that sickness was increased by partial starvation and the sick troops coming back . . . blocked the transport and consumed the supplies intended for those at the front.' Maybe the price paid for the strategic advantage of pushing on from Handeni was too high.

Smuts' staff were quick to criticise his method of command. He was always well forward, often with the advance guard in the firing line, and this tended to affect his judgement of the campaign as a whole because he became too involved with local situations. On the other hand, his official biographer emphasises the fact that 'the risks which he ran with his life and his constant determination to see with his own eyes were essential factors for his brand of leadership in these difficult situations. Smuts appreciated that 'leadership and drive were the supreme requisites of the campaign' in which the really dangerous enemy was sickness, slovenliness and the idleness that tropical Africa brings out. If the commander did not provide the drive and energy, who else would?

His Chief of Intelligence probably makes an accurate assessment of Smuts after lunching with him at Handeni: 'the more I see of the little man the more I like him. He has great charm and he has already won my affection. Always cheerful, witty and prepared to make the best of things. He is of course, no soldier, for as 'Truth' said some weeks back he is an amateur. His knowledge of human nature, his eye for country, his exceptional power of imposing his will on others, his remarkable personality, reckless disregard of difficulties and his very remarkable brain, compel one to respect him and admire him. Perhaps it is wrong to say he is no soldier. He is a bad tactician and strategist, an indifferent general, but in many ways a remarkable soldier.'

Smuts' force stopped during July 1916: the second phase of his plan had come to a close. His strategy had misled Lettow Vorbeck by adopting a double thrust and a vast area of German East Africa was now in British hands. But the Germans had suffered no major tactical defeat and their commander had held together his

A map by a veteran (A Buchanan of the 25th Royal Fusiliers) of the small but successful action against the Germans at Lukigura on the way to Morogoro, 24th June 1916

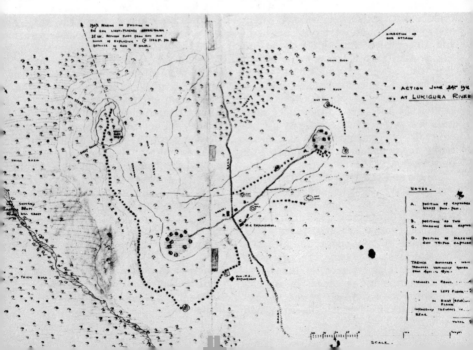

force, and their morale was high in spite of the tactical withdrawals. Moreover, he had diverted from the European theatre of war manpower and resources, and this had been his long term strategy from the start of the war.

By the third week in July, van Deventer and the 2nd Division were ready to resume the advance. Lettow Vorbeck had been forced to recall most of his troops from Kondoa Irangi to counteract Smuts' advance from Handeni. Lettow clearly stated his own problems when he wrote: 'I ask the reader to imagine himself in the position of a commander, with insufficient means, exposed to attack by superior numbers, who has continually to ask himself, what must I do in order to retain freedom of movement and hope.'

Van Deventer's task was not only to occupy the central railway but to move his force eastwards so as to co-operate more closely with Smuts' force. The 2nd Division was split into various forces, the cavalry went in a south-easterly direction, the infantry immediately south, and the two smaller columns cleared the right flank. Once again the German askaris withdrew skilfully and were not caught in van Deventer's thrusts. Dodoma, on the central railway, was occupied on 29th July, the Motor Cycle Corps finding the town evacuated and a white flag flying from its *Boma*. Van Deventer now had a stretch of one-hundred miles of the railway in his control; he concentrated his forces ready for a thrust eastwards to join up with Smuts.

Smuts and the 1st and 3rd Divisions were to have a harder advance to the railway, for they were faced by the Nguru Mountains and numerous streams. Smuts was still in personal command of the operation and the division had been reorganised. Throughout the period of inactivity the Germans had pounded the British positions with the long range *Königsberg* guns. The logistic backing had

now been resolved and Smuts decided to advance. The overall plan envisaged was a wide flanking movement by the 3rd Division, while the 1st East African Brigade under Sheppard was to hold the Germans frontally. For this type of attack to be successful it was essential for the front to be firmly held while the flanking movement got underway.

Sheppard's column did not succeed in the essential holding action, consequently the ambitious flanking movement came to nothing, and the German forces again slipped away undefeated. Smuts was now beginning to realise that Lettow Vorbeck had no intention of standing and fighting on a prepared defensive position.

To advance to Morogoro was to be the next objective of the 1st and 3rd Divisions. Smuts still held the view that he could hold Lettow Vorbeck, while van Deventer's force came from the German's flank and rear and thereby defeat the elusive German commander. Lettow Vorbeck held different views: 'the enemy expected us to stand and fight a final decisive engagement near Morogoro. To me, this idea was never altogether intelligible. Being so very much the weaker party, it was surely madness to await at this place the junction of the hostile columns, of which each one individually was already superior to us in numbers, and then fight with our back to the steep and rocky mountains.'

Van Deventer's 2nd Division advanced along the railway towards Kilosa through some of the most difficult country encountered in the campaign, being shelled the whole time by another of the *Königsberg*'s guns. The Official History says 'a gruelling phase of the operation was over. By dint of hard dogged marching, climbing and fighting the South Africans of the 2nd Division under

Armoured cars were used at Lukigura to pin the Germans down frontally while a flying column executed a flanking move

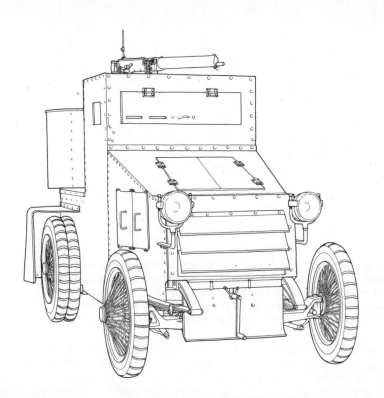

The Rolls-Royce armoured cars used by the British in East Africa were similar to the 1914 Admiralty pattern armoured cars, but did not have armour on the roof, as this was found to make the cars unendurably hot inside. *Weight :* 3.4 tons. *Length :* 16½ feet. *Width :* 6.25 feet. *Height :* 7½ feet. *Speed :* 50mph. *Armour :* 8mm maximum. *Armament :* One .303-inch Vickers machine gun. *Crew :* 3 (more armed men could be carried in the open back of the car). *Power :* Rolls-Royce engine, 40/50hp

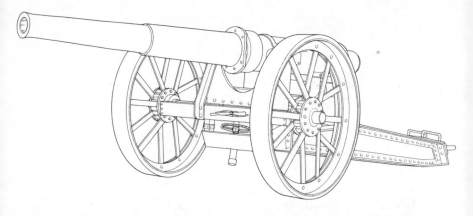

With the bottling up of *SMS Königsberg* in the delta of the Rufiji river, it was decided to remove her 105mm (4.1-inch) guns and mount them on improvised carriages, such as the British had made for use in the Boer War, to increase the artillery available to Lettow Vorbeck. *Calibre :* 4.13-inches. *Barrel length :* 40 calibres. *Weight of shell :* 30.86lbs. *Muzzle velocity :* 2,835 feet per second

steadily increasing hardship, as the line of communication lengthened, had pushed back the opposing Germans through sixty miles of most difficult hill country between Chunya and Kilosa, suffering a minimum of battle casualties but at the cost of reducing men and horses alike to utter exhaustion.'

South of Morogoro were the Uluguru Mountains and Smuts attempted, by converging the attacks of the 2nd Division and his own force, to trap Lettow Vorbeck with his back against the mountains. On 26th August the Rhodesians and the Baluchis entered Morogoro. The German force, as was becoming all too familiar, had slipped away.

The British forces now held the central railway. This was the great goal of Smuts' strategy and to achieve this result he had stretched his force to the limit. 'It may be said that I expected too much of my men, and that I imposed too hard a task on them under the awful conditions of this tropical campaigning. I do not think so. I am sure it was not possible to conduct this campaign successfully in

any other way. Hesitation in taking risks, slower moves, closer inspection of these auspices would only have meant the same disappearance of my men from fever and other tropical diseases, without any corresponding compensation to show in the defeat of the enemy and the occupation of his country.'

During 1915, while the British were on the defensive, the Belgian desire for joint operations was not fulfilled. Continuous Anglo-Belgian co-operation had seemed well nigh impossible in spite of the occasional conferences. But by 1916, the Belgian authorities were contemplating offensive action in an effort to gain complete control of Lake Tanganyika and to expand their territory through Ruanda – Urundi as far as Lake Victoria. So in 1916 Smuts had sent Brigadier-General Sir Charles Crewe, a South African politician, to maintain close liaison with General Tombeur, the Belgian commander.

The Belgians had raised a force of some 15,000 men, and Sir Charles Crewe has under his command approximately 2,000 men, mainly KAR.

Their plan was to move round Lake Tanganyika and seize the Ruanda-Urundi area of the German colony and use this victory as a bargaining instrument with the Germans. The German forces in Western Command, as it was known, were under command of Major-General Wahle. The general was a retired officer who had been visiting Dar es Salaam at the outbreak of hostilities and had offered his services to Lettow Vorbeck. He established his HQ at Tabora and had approximately 5,000 men under his command. His aim was not to defend his area permanently against the Belgians and British, but to withdraw and link up with Kraut and Lettow Vorbeck in the south-east of the colony.

The Belgians advanced slowly in Ruanda and Captain Wintgens, the German commander in the field, offered little resistance. It has been suggested that the Germans never had any intention of resisting the Belgians in Ruanda because they visualised this would be their only incursion into German East Africa. The further the Belgians advanced, the more isolated they became from their bases in the Congo. Their difficulties were compounded by their carrier corps problems, and Smuts' reluctance to help. Nevertheless, the Belgian occupation of Ruanda was complete by the end of May. To date, the British attitude had been defensive, but with the Belgian occupation of Ruanda-Urundi events took on a different complexion.

It appeared that the next logical step in the campaign was the seizure of Mwanza, but Tombeur had been ordered by his government to move against Kigoma and keep his command independent. Crewe decided therefore to act independently. Mwanza was evacuated by the Germans when they realised that there were two columns converging on the town. The British force was largely made up of the 4th KAR, which was in action for the first time as a battalion. The British Lake Force seized Mwanza on 14th July.

The camp at Morogoro. Smuts expected Lettow Vorbeck to stand and fight a decisive engagement here, but when the British arrived on 26th August 1916 they found that he had quietly slipped away

With the occupation of Mwanza the first stage of the long march to Tabora had been accomplished. An important area had been seized from the Germans with very few losses, but again the Germans had avoided battle and escaped virtually unscathed. Meanwhile the Belgians were advancing towards Kigoma, and by the end of the month had captured the town.

The operations of the two Allied commanders in this area were becoming more independent as the campaign progressed. The absence of communications, and a clash of personalities between Tombeur and Crewe accentuated the problem further. The advance to the railway and Tabora was to become an independent and uncoordinated scramble, with the Belgians advancing from Kigoma and the British from Mwanza. Crewe's force had to cover tough arid country and its progress was not unnaturally painfully slow. Their resupply problem was considerable.

The Belgian columns, on the other hand, had easier territory to cover,

Belgian native artillery. The Belgian role in Smuts' plan was to clear up the German forces in the north and west of the colony. By May 1916 their occupation of Ruanda was complete

lived off the land and were more dedicated to winning the race to Tabora. They arrived on the outskirts of Tabora where Wahle and a force containing two of the *Königsberg's* guns inflicted a sharp tactical defeat on them. The Germans then retired from Tabora in three columns towards Iringa, leaving behind 140 women and children in the care of the Governor's wife, Frau Ada von Schnee, a woman who then vowed never to speak to an Englishman again. The Governor himself determined to leave with the columns, forever conscious of his role as C-in-C. Lettow Vorbeck might have wished otherwise, that he should stay in the temporary capital and use his influence as Governor with the incoming Belgians for the protection of those left behind, for all the Germans were extremely fearful as to the treatment of the white residents by the victors in view of the atrocities committed by the German soldiery in occupied Belgium, strong rumours of which had flooded the Allies' ranks in spite of the dislocated communications. The Belgians occupied the town on 19th September. Some six days later Crewe's force reached Tabora.

The Belgians at this point had no further interest in following the

Sailors from the *Königsberg* man a machine gun. They were unused to bush fighting, and Northey's KAR askaris made short work of them in the push towards Iringa from the south

Germans; they had achieved all that their government required of them. In this epilogue to the scramble for Africa, the Belgians had seized Ruanda-Urundi. 'No Belgian interest now existed which would justify further Belgian participation in the campaign.' It was left to Crewe to push eastwards and link up with van Deventer, which he did by the end of September. His force was then disbanded, and Crewe himself returned to South Africa.

This small sideshow, predominately Belgian, had little military effect on the campaign as a whole, but a vast tract of territory had been won for Belgium. The seizure of the railway was complete and the Allied commander now had no worries about the northern part of German East Africa. But pressing southwards were three comparatively large German columns commanded by General von Wahle and Captains von Langenn and Wintgens.

The Nyasaland-Rhodesia Field Force, commanded by Brigadier-General Northey, numbered some 3,000 men, comprised of the 1st KAR, 1st and 2nd SA Rifles and companies of the BSA Police and Northern Rhodesia Police. This small force, striking into the south of the German colony, was to become 'the anvil of Smuts'hammer descending from the North', a difficult task for such a small force. The first phase of Northey's plan was to capture Neu Langenburg, the German district HQ. His force divided into four columns and advanced into German territory. The town was entered on 29th May and quantities of supplies and ammunition were taken. He then decided to move his HQ into Neu Langenburg and plan the next phase of the operation, the advance to Iringa. Smuts had ordered that Northey's force would best assist the main thrusts by 'an advance to Iringa to block the enemy's escape in that direction.' Northey had a formidable problem in commanding non-regular units and it is of interest to see

101

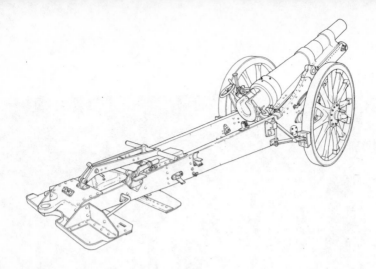

The German 1904 10.5cm field gun. *Calibre :* 10.5cm (4.13-inches). *Barrel length :* 30 calibres. *Gun weight :* 26½cwt. *Carriage weight :* 27¾cwt. *Weight limbered up :* 69cwt. *Elevation :* −5° to 30°. *Traverse :* 3°59′. *Weight of round :* 53lbs. *Weight of shell :* 39.5lbs. *Weight of charge :* 5lbs. *Muzzle velocity :* 1,830 feet per second. *Range :* 11,264 yards

in what detail he personally recorded for the benefit of his sub-unit commanders. In his 'instructions to commanders' he states 'every little detail must be brought out before hand, transport, supply, ammunition, bombs, entrenching tools (every man should carry at least a native hoe), medical stores, stretcher bearers, signallers and their gear.'

The next phase was to advance towards Iringa. The 1st KAR marched over the cold windswept plateau picking up straggling porters and abandoned stores en route, but the German rearguards escaped at the final moment and so avoided capture. The progress of the march was good, but as always the speed of the advance outstripped the supply columns. At this juncture, Northey decided to build up a firm base with supplies before pushing forward.

There were two routes from Neu Langenburg to Iringa and it was at this point that the German positions were held by a party of over one-hundred officers and men from the *Königsberg*. The KAR askaris made short work of the German sailors in

the unfamiliar bush fighting. On 24th July, Northey's small force came against a prepared defensive position at Malangali, but the gallant action of the KAR ensured success, the German force retreating and leaving their 10.5cm howitzer behind. By this time Northey's small column had advanced far into German territory, and of all the invading columns his was the only one which had any real cause to fear a German counteroffensive. Both his flanks were exposed, and he was aware of the dangerous situation in which his forces were placed. All the new recruits posted to the 1st KAR were now used to guard the extended lines of communication and complete their recruit training in the process, an ingenious solution to a difficult problem.

As Smuts pushed towards Morogoro it appeared that the Germans' line of retreat would be towards Mahenge instead of Iringa. Nonetheless, Northey's column continued towards Iringa and entered it on 29th August. He was now effectively contributing to the course of events in the north, as his actions were fitting into Smuts' overall plan of attacking the German forces from all directions. The effect of Northey's advance on the Africans was interesting. 'The defeat of the enemy at Malangali and the loss of their big gun has had an enormous effect on the Wahehe tribe, whose territory we are just penetrating; they would rise at once if they thought they could help us drive the enemy out, but as they are only armed with spears they cannot do much.' Northey's war diary tells only half the story; some years before the Germans had slaughtered much of the Wahehe tribe in an uprising and had taken the skull of the African Chief to Hamburg for the museum. There was little sympathy for the Germans in this area.

By now the supply line was 200 miles long from Northey's base on Lake Nyasa; a small German force in his rear could unbalance his command. The news of Wahle's withdrawal southwards from Tabora accentuated this possibility. But by pushing forward to Iringa, Northey prevented Kraut's retreating companies from entering the healthier area of Iringa and forced them towards Mahenge. The Official History states: 'By the end of Sep-

tember, Northey's small force 3,800 in all, opposed to German numbers steadily increasing towards parity if not superiority, stood facing eastwards dispersed along a front of 200 miles from Songea to Iringa, with its far-stretched lines of communications barely protected, with no general reserve and no prospect of further reinforcement. A precarious situation to which only the eventual arrival of van Deventer's troops from the north could bring relief . . . To their persistence and determination in a long and disappointing pursuit, to their steadfastness against constant hardships, high tribute is due.'

Considering the great distance that separated Northey's command from the main army, it was a considerable achievement on his part to maintain contact with Smuts. Even more notable was his ability to move his force so that it fitted in with the broader pattern of events. It is seldom

HMS Challenger, part of the combined naval and military force which by September 1916 had seized all the ports on the German East African coast

that an independent commander many miles from HQ has the foresight to sacrifice personal aim for the benefit of the overall plan.

As Smut's advance progressed, it was logical to seize the major ports on the coast of German East Africa, for this to some extent would ease the critical supply problem.

Bagamoyo was captured on 15th August by a combined naval and military force under the command of Rear-Admiral Charlton, who landed a party of marines and Zanzibar Rifles about 300-strong to seize the old Arab town. A stout defence was put up by Captain Bock von Wilfingen and the German askaris, but, considering the attacking force, they had little chance of holding the town. A naval squadron consisting of the battleship *Vengeance*, the cruiser *Challenger*, the monitors *Mersey* and *Severn* with the armed tug *Helmuth* were anchored off Bagamoyo to support the landing. Opposition came from an unexpected quarter; a *Königsberg* gun opened up on the fleet – yet again this destroyed cruiser was affecting the campaign. It is interesting to pause at this point to remember Lettow Vorbeck's strategic aim of attracting into East Africa the maximum numbers of British forces which could have been employed in more important theatres. This vast array of British naval power to capture such a small town was indeed just what he wanted.

With Bagamoyo captured, preparations now began for the conquest of Dar es Salaam, the capital of German East Africa. Brigadier-General Edwards assembled a force of about 2,000 and proceeded to march in a double thrust towards Dar es Salaam supported by the Royal Navy. The weather was very hot and humid, and Admiralty records state that the 2nd West Indian Regiment was so desperate with thirst and hunger that it consumed all the 12,000 gallons of water landed for the whole of the force!

The town was entered on 4th September by the 129th Baluchis, the German defenders having withdrawn. In subsequent proceedings in the Admiralty prize court, Dar es Salaam was adjudged to have been a naval capture and £100,000 prize money was awarded to the Royal Navy.

As the German forces were withdrawing into the south-east of the colony, Smuts realised that the seizure of the southern coastal ports was vital if the British supply routes were to be shortened. Smuts decided that the whole coastline was to be occupied and Kilwa should be the first to be tackled. The 2nd West Indian Regiment landed without incident, and the other ports were captured by a force commanded by Major Tyndall. Mikindani and Lindi were taken without difficulty. The whole coastline was now in British hands.

With all the harbours in British possession, work began on the development of Dar es Salaam as a supply base. The railway was of utmost importance and to have it working as far as Kilosa and Morogoro would have a considerable effect on Smuts' force. Van Deventer was still being resupplied overland from Mombasa via Taveta, Moshi and Kondoa Irangi. With the seizure of these ports the German commander must have surely realised that there was now absolutely no possibility of outside help.

After reaching Morogoro despite the total exhaustion of his troops and the skilful escape of the German forces yet again, Smuts was determined to continue a dual advance round the Uluguru Mountains. This was without doubt one of the most difficult operational areas of the whole campaign. Transport was ordered back to Morogoro and the South Africans forced their way south without blankets, great coats, food, porters or information. It was obvious that Lettow Vorbeck had withdrawn his force to Kisaki where he had assembled supplies and stores.

It is interesting to speculate at this point on the exercise of command in the German force. For nearly one year

now the African soldiers, led by their German officers, had been withdrawing and yet their morale was high and they were still a well organised army. The greatest single factor in war is morale; it has been said that morale is to the physical as three is to one, and here surely was proof of what a small force with high morale could achieve. The credit for producing this situation must understandably go to Lettow Vorbeck himself, and this campaign must stand as one of the First World War's most notable object lessons in maintaining morale.

Smuts' plan was to envelop the Uluguru Mountains by pushing the 1st Division round the eastern side and part of the 3rd Division round the western side. This plan inevitably meant sacrificing one of the cardinal rules of war – concentration of force to achieve victory – and left the Allied force open to defeat in detail. The German commander had observed the error: 'I waited at Kisaki with the main body, in order to be able quickly to recognise and make use of any favourable opportunity. As was to be expected, the enemy had, owing to

The destruction of the dock installations at Dar es Salaam by the Germans prior to evacuation

our withdrawal to Kisaki, abandoned his concentration on Morogoro, he had sent a few detachments direct over the Uluguru Mountains, but his other columns had separated and followed us extending far to the east and west. The hope of being able to defeat one or more of these columns separately was fulfilled beyond expectation.'

The German rear guards were well prepared. The 57th Wilde's Rifles and the Gold Coast Regiment bore the brunt of the initial thrusts round the mountains. The latter had made its name in the Cameroons where it was the first British unit in the whole war to go into action against the Germans. The total absence of reliable maps and information, together with difficulty in radio communications, made the brigade commanders' tasks impossible. They were attempting flanking moves with totally exhausted men and dying horses, a tactic which had not yet succeeded in the campaign. Lettow Vorbeck did not let the oppor-

Radio communications, as yet still chronically unreliable. This factor, compounded with the almost total absence of reliable maps and information, made the brigade commanders' tasks near impossible

tunity slip from his grasp. 'The gallant 11th Field Company, under Lieutenant Volkein, worked through the dense bush close up to the out-flanking enemy, and immediately attacked with bayonet, cheering. With that, the enemy's beautiful plans completely collapsed, our further advance simply rolled him up, and he was completely defeated.'

In the pursuit of such an indefatigable enemy, the task demanded of British troops might appear to be more than they could tackle. Various diaries reveal the disenchantment with which the soldier sometimes viewed the campaign, now reduced to an almost continual hunt for a will-o'-the-wisp opponent. At times, coupled with the expected privations of the fighting man overseas, the tropical climate magnified his troubles which were compounded by the inconsiderate attitudes of superior officers.

A particularly telling extract from the diary of Lance-Corporal Hopper of the 25th Royal Fusiliers (Legion of Frontiersmen) is indicative of the depression and low spirits which pervaded some Allied contingents at times: 'We are getting any amount of wild animal's flesh to eat but we don't want it – it is the other things we want. I took twelve jiggers out this morning – I think that is about the average each day! I think it is time they sent us on a sea trip (home) for the good of our health, I think all they are bothering about is seeing who can get the most honours and decorations amongst the South Africans.'

Meinertzhagen also confirms this

attitude in a rather humorous account of the awarding of Russian decorations: 'A large batch of Russian decorations arrived last mail for distribution. There is naturally much grumbling at the method employed in their distribution, for nearly every recipient is a South African. Old van Deventer was given the plum, the order of St Vladimir. On receiving it he wired to Smuts in great indignation, as he had been told that St Vladimir ranked after St Anne. But as Smuts assured him that St Vladimir was the prize and very distinguished, van Deventer wires "Please convey my thanks to the Tsar." '

Lance-Corporal Hopper continues in his own descriptive way: 'I do not care to grouse in this diary although I feel I would like to do so many a time, but we have to put up with things even after we have our grouse and I have not much space to spare – there are oft times I would like to speak about which are very galling to us seeing we are all human beings. One part of our orders given to the Company Orderly Sergeant last night referring to the distribution of native carriers on trek (as we have no motors or wagons) reads as follows: 20 British officers – 4 porters each (80); 300 Rank and file – 96 porters (96). This allows one porter for three men. That allows the officers to live in luxury where as we have all our equipment to carry and sometimes they give us two or three days' rations to carry on us to save carriers carrying them for us, and the officers carry nothing except a revolver and have white servants and cooks as well as black servants. We have been allowed a native *toto* (boy) not a man as they want men as carriers, these boys can't carry anything for us except perhaps a billycan but they are handy for fetching water, wood and making a drop of

Native porters carrying supplies. In addition to those in the British Carrier Corps, the British troops were allowed approximately one porter for every three men

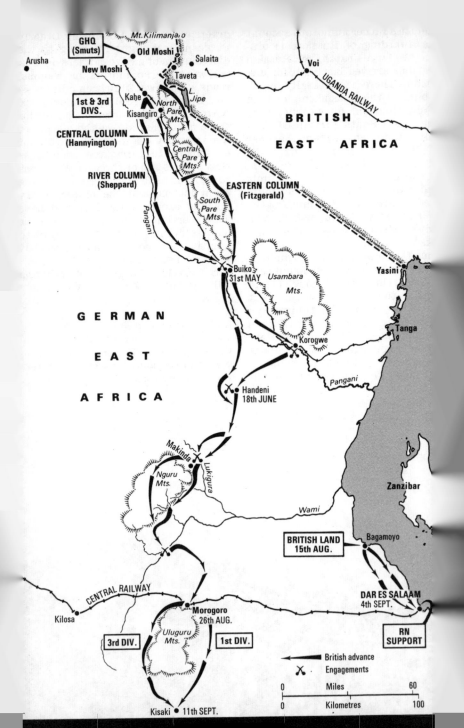

British advance from Moshi 1916

tea. To this boy they compel us to pay five rupees a month and keep him out of our small rations or buy mealie for him. We also have to find him an old blanket or something to let the poor little devil lay on as they have no clothing only the bits we give them and we have to be careful what we give them or we get into trouble for disposing of government property. Yesterday they paraded all the officers' boys, we were told that they would be rationed and would get *posho* and the other poor devils would get nothing only what we can ill afford to give out of our very scanty rations. Another small item here is they issued us all with a water *chargill* (canvas carrier) a short while ago but they have collected them all in again except one to four men for reserve water that is alright for an attack but the water is a long distance to fetch and only having one *chargill* for four keeps us or the *toto* continually fetching it, as this only holds 7/8 pints when full and there is always about two pints leak out. That means although good water is plentiful we are situated here with nothing to fetch it in – there are hundreds of other instances like these I could mention.'

On 11th September General Brits' force, famished and worn out, entered Kisaki, and the Allied force had linked up on the south of the mountain range. The 2nd Division had worked southwards from Kilosa and van Deventer had personally taken control. They fared no better than any other part of the British force. The stoical General Benange stated in an operation report, 'I cannot too strongly emphasise the arduous nature of these operations, the troops being compelled to climb ridge and mountain through bush, heavy grass and *dongas* often without food and without opportunities of cooking even when rations were issued.'

Lettow Vorbeck, while making the most of the British mistakes, had problems of his own: 'the troops were very fatigued and several people were suffering badly from nerves.' His African troops were falling asleep standing up.

The British forces had succeeded in taking the Uluguru Mountains area and both columns which had gone round either side of the mountain had linked up at Kisaki. By the end of September, Smuts' command could move no further. Transport and supply difficulties had become insuperable, and the troops, worn out by incessant hardship and disease, could do no more. The British forces in East Africa had come to a standstill.

On 30th September 1916 Smuts wrote to Governor Schnee, 'In spite of the conspicuous ability and bravery of the German defence the end could only be deferred at the cost of terrible losses and suffering,' the time had come 'to consider very seriously whether this useless resistance could not now cease in a manner honourable.' Lettow Vorbeck's reaction to this was predictable. 'General Smuts realised that his blow had failed. He sent me a letter calling upon me to surrender, by which he showed that as far as his force was concerned he had reached the end of his resources.'

By the end of September 1916 the campaign, costly beyond all expectations in men and material, disappointing in its total results, had made some progress before coming once more to a standstill. It had changed from a boldly planned offensive at the beginning of the year to a struggle of attrition.

Smuts had gained the central railway, the German capital, a vast tract of German East Africa and all the sea ports, but he had failed to defeat the German forces in a tactical battle. Lettow Vorbeck was still at large and prepared to go on fighting. The aim of all war is the destruction of the enemy; the British had failed to crush a far smaller force who had no hope of reinforcement or help.

The German commander had maintained and succeeded in his aim; the diversion of the maximum amount of

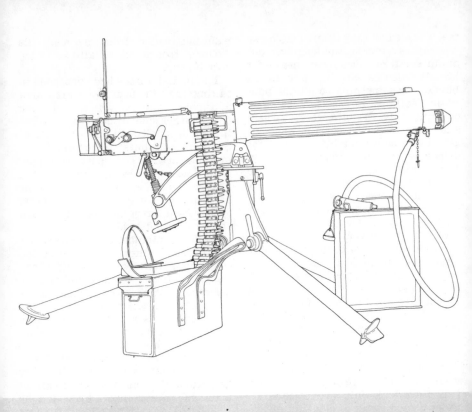

The Vickers .303-inch Machine Gun Mark I was the standard machine gun in use by British forces in both world wars, and was a sturdy (if heavy) and reliable weapon. It is shown mounted on a Mark IVB tripod. *Calibre :* .303-inch. *Method of operation :* Recoil with gas boost from a muzzle booster. *Weight of gun :* 33lbs (without water). *Weight of tripod :* 50lbs. *Coolant :* Water (7lbs in weight). *Length :* 43 inches. *Barrel length :* 28.4 inches. *Ammunition supply :* Canvas belts, each holding 250 rounds. *Muzzle velocity :* 2,440 feet per second. *Cyclic rate of fire :* 450-550 rounds per minute

British equipment and men from the European theatre to the less important East African campaign. Lord Kitchener appeared to be the only Allied leader who appreciated the strength of General von Lettow Vorbeck's strategy. His view was that Smuts should have stopped when he had secured the Kilimanjaro area and eliminated all prospects of invasion from German East Africa.

Smuts had been anxious to avoid casualties and had executed a series of turning movements which, because of his overwhelming numerical superiority, forced the Germans to withdraw. Never once did he inflict a tactical defeat on the German commander, but casualties from disease and the breakdown of the logistic system brought him to a halt. The ever-growing Allied army was becoming an embarrasment, not an advantage; it could not be moved rapidly or maintained adequately. From the point of view of tactics, the lessons of bush warfare had to be learnt by hard experience. Fighting what might be termed a continuous night operation at short range made

The machine gun had proved to be the dominant weapon in this campaign, partly owing to the peculiar conditions of fighting in the bush which (like night operations) has the effect of causing rifle fire to go high

ambush and surprise easy and protection virtually impossible.

The machine gun, as on the Western Front, proved to be the dominant weapon, for rifle fire (as in night operations) was always high and not effective; on the other hand, the bayonet was suprisingly effective in this campaign.

'The morale factor must be kept in mind more constantly in tropical Africa than elsewhere. There can be no doubt that the long spells without recreation, much less leave, and without letters and news, told as heavily on the spirit of the troops as did the privations.' The greatness of General von Lettow Vorbeck is clearly brought out by this quote from the British Official History. His ability to maintain the morale of a small army, cut off from all supplies, news and letters, waging a constant fighting withdrawal, must rank as one of the major command achievements in the First World War and become an object lesson to military historians of the importance of morale in war.

The British army had to be reshaped because, weakened by months of semi-starvation, exhausted by endless weeks of marching, the troops (the South Africans in particular) were falling sick in such numbers that the hospitals were overflowing and the field units were becoming a mere skeleton force. Only the African askaris of the KAR were capable of fighting in this type of war successfully, and these wonderful soldiers were from now onwards to come into their own and form the major part of the British force.

The campaign had lost all momentum. The army had to be reformed, South African and British battalions sent home for a rest, the logistic system completely overhauled, and many new battalions of the KAR raised in order to form the spearhead of the next phase. Lettow Vorbeck had successfully withdrawn his force, and he was determined to fight on for as long as the war lasted.

Escape into Portuguese East Africa

By September 1916 Smuts was forced to call a halt to his advance. His lines of communication had become so stretched that his logistic organisation was hard pressed to carry out its task. But more important, the European and South African troops were finding it almost impossible to continue in the harsh African climate. The period from September 1916 to November 1917 saw the occupation of German territory completed largely by the efforts of the KAR and West African units, and yet Lettow Vorbeck, the master of the fighting withdrawal, still had not been brought to battle or decisively defeated.

The months of October, November and December were months of reorganisation, and the expansion of the KAR was given utmost priority. The Official History clearly stated the advantages of the African soldier: 'There stood out, too, the further distinguishing peculiarity of a climate pitilessly hostile not only to the European but to the Indian soldier, and in particular, in this connection, the rainy season, which while it lasts, not only takes its heavy toll of health, but renders serious military operations a physical impossibility. To defeat the climate little regard had been paid, yet here above all lay the

The *Schutztruppe,* with its artillery, is inexorably pushed back into the south-eastern corner of the colony

real reason why, in the end, the valour and steadfast endurance of the troops from the United Kingdom and the British Dependancies elsewhere were of no avail to keep them in the field. Only the African soldier could stand the East African climate indefinitely.'

When Smuts took stock of the situation and realised that most of his white troops were unfit for further action, he said 'I believe between

Left: Wounded men of the Nigerian Brigade. By September 1916 Smuts had to call a halt because he was outrunning his logistic backing, and because sickness was having a disastrous effect on the military value of his European and Indian troops. *Below:* KAR recruits are kitted out. The KAR was slow to expand before 1916 largely because of unwillingness to accept the fact that the black soldier was better than the white under East African conditions

October and December 1916 we evacuated between 12,000–15,000 patients, malaria cases mostly. Nothing could show more eloquently the deadly nature of the country into which we had now moved.'

The fluctuations in the strength of the 2nd Loyal North Lancashire Regiment illustrates how the British troops had suffered. In November 1914 its strength was 832 all ranks; by 10th June 1915 only 350 were fit for active service; on 31st October the regiment was sent to South Africa to recuperate and returned in June 1916 with 531 all ranks. By December the unit had fallen to 345 all ranks in spite of the fact that it had not seen heavy fighting. The 2nd Rhodesian Regiment, strength 500 in March 1915, was by October 1916 down to 125, and by December only sixty-seven remained. During the period March 1915 to January 1917, a total of 1,038 of all ranks served with the unit. Recorded casualties were: killed thirty-six, wounded eighty-four, admissions to hospital 2,272, total cases of sickness 10,626 (3,127 malaria, 921 dysentery). Indian troops also suffered similar casualties to the white troops, and like the KAR had borne the brunt of some of the heaviest fighting. Medical boards were now set up during this period of reorganisation. As a result, over 12,000 South Africans were sent home. Replacements had to be found from somewhere.

The expansion of the KAR had been slow to start. As far back as 1914 it had been recognised as the obvious solution by some of the more farsighted British officers, but failure and indeed almost incredible stubborness to accept the fact that the black soldier was better than the white in East African conditions prevented recruiting and enlargement. During the period October 1916 to November 1917, all recruiting was centralised and much was done to rationalise the training of the KAR. Differences of pay and conditions were smoothed out and the number of British NCOs serving with KAR battalions was increased.

Colonel E H Llewellyn, who was appointed Commandant of the KAR, was responsible for the introduction of the new training schemes which were to equip the African askari for his arduous role.

As the KAR was to play such an important part in the remainder of the campaign, it is essential to look a little more closely at its organisation. Between 1st January 1916 and 1st July 1917 the force expanded from 4,338 to 23,978. In the early part of 1917 the KAR consisted of five regiments, each with its own depot, totalling altogether thirteen battalions. But in February 1917 it was agreed to increase the KAR to twenty battalions and in April 1917 the formation of KAR began at Morogoro, initially using ex-German askaris who were in the prisoner-of-war camps. The KAR Official History comments: 'At first the quality of these new units was very different from that of the three battalions that had participated in the campaign to date . . . So much the greater therefore was the achievement of those officers, NCOs and experienced soldiers who carried the new battalions through the disasters that befell some of them during their first few months on active service.'

It was indeed a fatal error on the part of the British command that it had not appreciated the ability of the African soldier earlier, for it would undoubtedly have saved the vast wastage in men and materials which epitomised the first two years of the campaign. What was more logical than to conduct the fight against Lettow Vorbeck with the same type of soldier that he himself was using? It obviously would have released many more South African and British regiments for other important theatres of war more suited to their physical makeup.

Meinertzhagen had seen service with the KAR between 1902 and 1906 and was very aware of the great potential of these soldiers. His comments substantiate this: 'Another error we made was not raising a division of Kings African Rifles as soon as war was declared. Now that it is too late we are doing it. For this error Governor Belfield and the Colonial Office are responsible. We put it to them on many occasions. Early in 1915 Wapshare made definite plans for the raising of a KAR division, but the Governor and the Colonial Office turned it down. Graham was against it on the grounds that suitable recruits would not be forthcoming. I did not agree with this view and I have been proved right, for we now have a division of King's African Rifles, consisting of excellent material but not yet fully trained. Their weakness lies in their British officers, who naturally are not up to the standard of prewar officers. I believe that if by the end of 1915 we had had a well trained division of KAR we could have accomplished as much and more than we have done since Smuts and his South Africans arrived, and at less than half the cost. But jealousy and apathy stopped the scheme.'

During September 1916 British troops were dispatched to Kilwa. The reason behind this move was to strike at the German food supply depots which were becoming increasingly scarce, and also to effect another turning movement against Lettow Vorbeck. A defensive position was prepared on the heights overlooking Kilwa and by the end of September four battalions had arrived. Smuts had given orders that the Kilwa Force should push inland as soon as possible. Brigadier-General Hannyington who commanded the Kilwa Force set out for Kibata with a detachment of 2nd KAR, and Kibata Fort was seized on 18th October. This was a real baptism of fire for the new KAR army.

At the end of October, Smuts visited Kilwa and decided that the HQ of 1st Division, together with the 2nd Infantry Brigade, should go to Kilwa, and by the end of November the Kibata garrison had been strengthened. Between 6th and 9th December Lettow Vorbeck attacked the Kibata gar-

rison. He opened his attack by shelling the fort with a 4.1-inch *Königsberg* gun, a 4.1-inch howitzer and a field gun. In all some 300 shells fell on the British positions. The heavy artillery concentration (heavy, that is, for East Africa) was a severe test for some of the new British askaris and they had difficulty in maintaining their defensive positions. As a result Lettow Vorbeck's attack was successful. The young askaris in the KAR were not used to the severity of the struggle and the German attack inflicted heavy losses on the KAR and the Gold Coast Regiment. Lettow Vorbeck appreciated the strategic effects of this small engagement: 'Our vigorous actions at Kibata forced him [*the British*] to move from Kilwa against us and to leave the rest of the country and our supply system in peace.'

The provision of food was becoming a major concern of Lettow Vorbeck's mobile defence. His African troops were easy to feed. Maize was the basic food required, but to obtain adequate

The *Königsberg*'s 4.1-inch guns turned up once again at Fort Kibata to shell a detachment of Hannyington's force on 6th December

supplies needed careful consideration of the location of the maize plantations. The German commander had to site and organise the planting of maize in locations which would remain free of war until it had matured and ripened and was ready for consumption. The co-ordination of the availability of food supplies with the conduct of his mobile defensive actions was a significant indication of his ability as a commander. To maintain a reasonably large force in such hostile conditions was a great problem, and although it is always emphasised that the Germans worked on interior lines of communication which made their logistic backing easier to handle, they still had to provide food for their army. It must be remembered that Lettow Vorbeck received no supplies from outside German East Africa and had

117

to plan his withdrawal in conjunction with availability of food.

It is interesting to note that he learned at about this time that he had been awarded the Pour le Mérite, the German equivalent of the Victoria Cross. The news was received in a personal letter from General Smuts! Lettow Vorbeck records: 'He expressed the hope that his cordial congratulations would not be unacceptable to me. I thanked him equally politely, although at first I believed that he was confusing it with the Second Class of the Order of the Crown with swords which I received a short time before. I mention this letter from General Smuts as a proof of the mutual personal esteem and chivalry which has existed throughout in spite of the exhausting warfare carried on by both sides.' This was undoubtedly a unique campaign in the history of the First World War.

The main force had stayed inactive on the banks of the Mgeta since September, but Smuts now activated it into four columns under Brigadier-Generals Sheppard, Beves, Cunliffe and Lyall, aimed at overwhelming the Germans on the line of the River Mgeta and simultaneously outflanking them and securing a crossing on the River Rufiji at Mkalinzo. Again the axiom of war – concentration of forces at one vital point – was ignored, and the price paid was that Lettow Vorbeck was not decisively defeated.

The columns advanced and Beves was given the task of executing the flanking move to cross the Rufiji. The

Top: A German supply column. Lettow Vorbeck's vigorous action against Kibata forced the British to move from Kilwa against him and thus distracted their attention from his supply system.
Left: A German native porters' encampment. Unable to get supplies from outside German East Africa, Lettow Vorbeck's efforts to coordinate the procurement of food with his mobile defensive tactics stretched his genius to the full

advance was slow, for the rains made it impossible to make any speed. In fact the Nigerians waded waist deep for most of the advance. Simultaneously with the four columns advancing, a further push was to be made from Kibata. After their initial success, the Germans had turned the positions at Kibata into a well defended locality and the subsequent Kibata battles were fought in conditions which resembled Flanders more than did any other engagement in East Africa. The familiar theme of rain, opposing trenches, sapping, sniping, periscopes and grenades were all to be found in this engagement.

Beves' column, which was composed mainly of South Africans, pushed its way through thick bush and reached the Rufiji. They encountered no opposition, crossed the river and dug in. The Germans were surprised at the sudden appearance of the South African troops. The other three columns reached the Rufiji and, skilfully under cover of darkness, established themselves on the German side of the river. But yet again, the Germans slipped through the net.

Smuts had reached the Rufiji, a notable achievement. But at this juncture, decimated by sickness, Beves' brigade was returned to the Union of South Africa together with many other South African troops, and this front was left mainly to the Nigerians. Smuts declared 'that the campaign was over, and that all that now remained to be done is to sweep up the remnants of the enemy force'! This was not an accurate or a widely-held belief. Lettow Vorbeck had still not been brought to battle and was still full of fight. The majority of German East Africa was undoubtedly now in British hands, but the war dragged on and the men Smuts saved from becoming battle casualties by his cautious approach became hospital casualties. 'Smuts was not an astute soldier; a brilliant statesman and politician, but no soldier' was Meinertzhagen's view.

This series of operations (the last, and in some respects the boldest of Smuts' plans) could hardly be said to have come within measurable distance of success. Smuts' converging advance from the north and 1st Division's from the south had nearly effected a junction which might have encircled the German main body on 'the Rufiji and compelled its surrender. But the defeat of the Germans was the paramount aim and this had still not been achieved.

By the beginning of February 1917 the rains had begun to fall with abnormal violence. All hopes of striking a final blow at the Germans vanished. The problems of food supply was acute on both sides. It became a war in which famine was frequent. Colonel Dobbs, the British AQMG, stated in his report 'I honestly cannot see how we are going to feed the troops in view of the weather and serious transport situation.' The Germans withdrew from the Rufiji delta, and fighting on this front came to halt during the wet season.

General Northey's force, which had pushed up from Rhodesia to Iringa, was by the end of September extended over a front some 200 miles wide. The 2nd Division under van Deventer had reached the railway and did not have the ability to go further south. Northey's position had become precarious for the German force which, retreating from Tabora commanded by Wahle, was marching eastwards in

Top left: **Brigadier-General Beves, commander of the column which pushed south over the Rufiji as part of Smuts' renewed offensive early in 1917.** *Left:* **Brigadier-General Cunliffe. His Nigerians were the major force left on the Rufiji front when Beves' brigade was returned to South Africa, decimated by sickness.** *Top right:* **The Nigerians wade waist deep in their advance in the Rufiji area.** *Right:* **3rd Battalion of the Nigerian Brigade and their native porters on a drier part of the Rufiji front**

three columns under Captains Wintgens, von Langenn and Zingel and was heading straight for Northey's line of communication. His force at Iringa was in danger of being isolated. Wahle's command was about 2,000-strong and in a good state of morale. He held the initiative, but his command structure was not strong and some of his subordinates acted independently, thereby taking away from his good tactical and strategic position.

The large force operating in the rear of the British positions at the time presented a very real threat, but because Wahle's aim was to withdraw and join up with Lettow Vorbeck the potential German threat was never fully realised. Yet his large force broke right across the British line of communication. Iringa was besieged and a substantial supply depot at Ngominji was taken, but not until it had put up a good fight. Wintgen's column, pushing southwards, surrounded Lupembe, but the steadiness of the KAR held the German attack.

It was now the turn of the British to attack. Wahle's rearguard of 300 men and a 4.1-inch howitzer were captured. The bulk of his force, however, had got through the British lines and had linked up with Major Kraut in the Mahenge area. Previously in December Smuts had been able to call upon Northey to support the general advance from the Mgeta River by pushing inland from Lupembe, and it was during this advance that his Intelligence system indicated that the German forces were pulling back. The problem in this area was again one of supplies and it seemed that only the Songea area was capable of supporting logistically the German force.

The KAR reach the Rufiji – only to find that once again Lettow Vorbeck had slipped away, so that although the majority of German East Africa was now in British hands, still he had not been brought to battle and decisively defeated

Captain Wintgens in General Wahle's column refused to join Lettow Vorbeck and had decided to wage a war of his own. His column fought several engagements against Northey's force and then, to everyone's amazement, he turned north towards Tabora. This caused great alarm in this Belgian-held town. By February it had become apparent that Wintgens was handling his force with considerable skill and, with the initiative firmly in his hands, he had pushed on, driving clean through the British lines of communication. By May the situation was such that a special force, commanded by Brigadier-General Edmunds and totalling 1,700 rifles and fourteen machine guns, was formed to track down Wintgens' small army. Fever eventually took toll of Wintgens' health and on 21st May he handed over command to Captain Naumann and he himself surrendered. Naumann took over command of the force numbering some fifty Europeans, 500 askaris and 700 carriers and continued to fight with renewed vigour and drive. He changed his direction of advance repeatedly, thereby causing danger to the Belgians and to British East Africa itself.

Naumann's force had by now moved up quite close to the border of British East Africa and was causing considerable alarm in the British colony and also among the Belgians in their newly-acquired territory. He was still actively patrolling and attacking in September 1917, but on 30th September he was finally surrounded by Colonel Lilley and a force of the 4th KAR quite close to the border of British East Africa. On 2nd October he formally surrendered with his little command of fourteen Europeans, 150 askaris and 300 carriers. For almost one year a British column had been kept in the field chasing this force over 1,600 miles, creating disorganisation and diverting valuable askaris from the main war theatre in the south.

Lettow Vorbeck is less complimentary, for he says: 'Captain Naumann led the forces on until finally he surrendered to the pursuing enemy column near Mt Kilimanjaro towards the end of 1917. It is to be regretted that this operation carried out with so much determination and initiative, became separated so far from the major theatre as to be of little use.'

Lettow Vorbeck's judgement is quite wrong on this little sideshow. His attitude is understandable because he had lost control of part of his army at a time when command and control must have been one of the most important factors in his ability to continue the war. To lose control of his scattered forces at this point would have spelled disaster and therefore he does not give this small German force credit for its incredible efforts. From the British point of view it had been a considerable danger operating in the rear of the main forces. Naumann had held the initiative and was completely independent for supply and thereby free to attack anywhere. Van Deventer, who had taken over command of the British Forces from General Hoskins, comments: 'Such a raid could perhaps only have been carried out in a country like German East Africa where the bush is often so thick that two considerable forces may pass within a mile of each other and where an energetic leader of a small force can nearly always live off the country.'

In January 1917 Smuts was called away from East Africa to represent South Africa at the Imperial Defence Conference in London. At this point it is opportune to assess Smuts' contribution to the campaign. The war in East Africa had been going on for nineteen months when Smuts arrived. This period was marked by failure, a static defence and the subsequent lowering of morale which results from lack of success. The war had opened with a resounding defeat for the British at Tanga; in all, a very poor showing was offered by the British generals in command at this time. Their quality and performance was probably at its lowest during the beginning of the campaign. During these months, the Germans on the whole had been superior to the British both in strategy and effective striking power, which says much for the defenders' comparatively sparse numbers. The German commander during 1915 used his force as a guerrilla command and struck again and again at the British life line, the Uganda railway which joined the interior of the British colony to the coast. His efforts were also concentrated on recruiting and training his African soldiers who were to fight throughout the entire campaign with him.

During November 1915 Smuts had been offered command of all troops in East Africa, but he had refused as he felt that the situation in South Africa needed his presence. The offer of this command by the British government may have come for two reasons; it may have been as a compliment to his past military achievements, or in deference to South Africa which would inevitably be supplying more and more men for the war. A politic appointment, it would mean that for the first time, Afrikaner and British would make common cause and weld the recent imperial tie in a joint campaign. It has already been recounted how when Smuts did not initially accept the appointment, General Smith-Dorien was appointed, and how when he was taken ill on the way to Cape Town Smuts was offered the job again. Thus on 10th February 1916 Smuts became the second youngest Lieutenant-General in the British army.

Brigadier-General Crowe, the commander of the British Artillery in East Africa, states: 'It was a bold stroke to entrust the command of these bodies of troops and the carrying out of these operations to a man who was not a soldier, who had practically no experience of handling any considerable force.' Lloyd George was succinct in his views about generals: 'there is no profession where ex-

Smuts (seated, far right) at the
Imperial Defence Conference in London,
January 1917. He was succeeded as
C-in-C by Hoskins, and then by van
Deventer

perience and training count less in
comparison with judgement and flair.'
Smuts certainly had flair. In the House
of Commons Mr Asquith said of the
new general, 'we can have the utmost
confidence in General Smuts, in view
of his varied military experience.'

With South African reinforcements,
Smuts arrived in Mombasa on 19th
February and immediately during his
first week in command he conducted a
most searching reconnaissance of the
weak spots of the German dispositions.
This in itself was a complete change
in the approach towards generalship
in East Africa. Commanders in the
past had not bothered much about
finding things out for themselves.
Smuts' enthusiasm and drive injected
new life into the British garrison.
Almost at a stroke he succeeded in
raising the morale of his army. No
general so far in East Africa had been
capable of doing this.

The result of Smuts' close examina-
tion of the situation was his accurate
assessment of the German position.
The gap between the Pare Mountains

and Kilimanjaro in which Taveta lay
and where the Germans had been forti-
fying themselves over the previous
year was the obvious gateway into the
German colony and the key to the
German forward positions. Smuts
states: 'This gap had to be forced at
whatever cost. I preferred to manoeuvre the enemy out of it. I advanced
the bulk of my force by night against
the enemy's left flank, took from him
the foothills of Kilimanjaro by surprise and within twenty-four hours
compelled him to evacuate his practically impregnable Taveta positions.'

This first move by Smuts, although
impressive, was not in military terms
as significant as it might appear. From
a military point of view, there is
confusion in Smuts statement: to
force the gap whatever the cost is not
compatible with outmanoeuvring the

Germans. A decisive victory was required and this would not be achieved by manoeuvre which implied lack of concentration at the vital point.

Meinhertzhagen continues the military assessment of Smuts. 'Would Smith-Dorrien have finished the campaign sooner than Smuts? – I reply to that, 'Smith-Dorrien would have finished the campaign at or near Taveta by capturing or signally defeating the enemy's main forces. He would have brought an overwhelming infantry and artillery concentration against the enemy and would have used his mounted troops in a wide sweeping movement from Longido aiming at getting astride the enemy's lines of communications. Our strategy was simple, our numbers vastly superior and Smith-Dorrien is not the man to miss his opportunities as did Smuts.'

Smuts had outmanoeuvred Lettow Vorbeck, but he had missed an opportunity to defeat the German forces in a decisive encounter. It can also be argued that Smuts was not prepared to fight the German commander on a defensive position of the German's own choosing, preferring to outflank him rather than to meet in a pitched battle. This assessment may be founded on some truth, but the facts are that a commander's aim must be to destroy the enemy. The longer he delays this the more casualties there will be, and this must be used as the measure of Smuts' opening stroke at the Germans. Smuts continues, 'Never had I seen so sudden and complete a transformation in the spirits of opposing forces; our men, who had retreated before the enemy in the confusion at Salaita Hill now advanced with dauntless élan against the hidden foe in the dense bush of the mountain slopes or the Ruvu swamps.'

It was indeed true that Smuts had revitalised the British forces, his magnetic personality and drive had transformed the army. Morale was raised at this point in the campaign to a high level by Smuts' own personal example. He was always to be found in the front line sharing the hardships with his troops, so much so that he was criticised for losing the overall picture of the campaign by becoming involved in minor episodes. Morale is the greatest single factor in war. Smuts appreciated this and did all in his power to see that the morale of his army was high. The views of a junior officer in the British force are revealing: 'The real history of the war begins with Smuts; for, prior to his coming we were merely at war; but when he came we began to fight. Wherever that rather short, but well-knit figure appeared, with his red beard, well streaked with grey, beneath the red staff cap, confidence reigned in all our troops. And to the end this trust has remained unabated.'

The British force was composed of units from India, Great Britain, South Africa and Kenya, comprising various races and numerous languages, and furthermore these units varied greatly in their professional ability, some being newly-raised African regiments, others well established British infantry regiments or British Volunteer Battalions. It is a mark of Smuts' greatness as a general that he managed to weld these vastly differing units into a united whole. His energy and drive were instrumental in achieving this favourable situation.

Smuts continued his offensive by planning an invasion of the German colony from various directions. 'Our object was not merely the defeat of the enemy, but the effective occupation of his huge territory in the shortest possible time.' He launched

Top: Smuts' camp just before he left for London in January – close to the front line. His willingness to suffer the hardships of the front along with his men had been one of the prime causes of the upturn in British morale after he assumed command. *Right:* A boxing match in the camp of the East African Mounted Rifles

his offensive from the north in two thrusts, one towards the railway via Kondoa Irangi, the other along the Usambara Mountains. Again he split his forces. The Germans were pushed back by overwhelming superiority but not defeated. A co-ordinated attack was executed from the west by the Belgians and from the south by General Northey. The British forces were closing in on Lettow Vorbeck's army, and it was an indication of Smuts' military ability that he could plan and co-ordinate these difficult thrusts. The result of his strategy was that by September 1916 two-thirds of the German territory had been occupied by the British. The central railway from Dar es Salaam to Lake Tanganyika was in British hands and no attempt was made by the Germans to double back and threaten the lines of communication.

Conditions became increasingly difficult as the campaign progressed. Smuts vividly describes this himself. 'It is impossible for those unacquainted with German East Africa to realise the physical, transport and supply difficulties of the advance over this magnificent country consisting of great mountain systems alternating with huge plains; with a great rainfall and wide, unbridged rivers in the regions of the mountains and insufficient surface water on the plains for the needs of an army, with magnificent bush and primeval forest everywhere, pathless, trackless, except for the spoor of elephant or the narrow footpaths of the natives; the malaria mosquito everywhere, everywhere belts infested with the deadly tsetse fly which make an end of all animal transport; the ground almost everywhere a rich black or red cotton soil

The new C-in-C, Lieutenant-General Hoskins. Smuts' comments to Hoskins on leaving for London were to the effect that the Germans had been defeated and all that now remained was a little clearing up. Hoskins was soon to learn otherwise

which any transport converts into mud in the rain or dust in the drought.'

Smuts realised the enormity of the logistic problems, but did not plan sufficiently to overcome its consequences. The advance and out-flanking moves he religiously followed placed an impossible strain on the administrative system and also on the health of his soldiers. A vicious circle was established, the stretched lines of communications made it impossible to feed the advancing troops who became sick and returned to the overcrowded hospitals. New recruits came forward unable to survive the severe conditions. The same happened to them. The losses in men and material in this campaign were vast. Inevitably this must indicate a weakness in Smuts' generalship.

When Smuts left for London most of the German colony was in British hands, but the price paid had been high. He had tried to avoid casualties particularly among the South Africans. This is understandable, for South Africa had just concluded some twelve years before a devastating war within her own frontiers against the British. Any further bleeding of her manhood could only harm her development as an emergent nation. Ironically, this desire to avoid casualties in pitched battles caused greater casualties from sickness and hunger. The state of protagonists after his ten months in command is aptly summed up by the British Official History: 'Yet still the enemy, in ever dwindling numbers, but handled with unfailing skill by a master of strategic retreat, remained in being.'

Lieutenant-General A R Hoskins was appointed the new C-in-C when Smuts left for London. His task was made more difficult by Smuts' farewell comments when he stated that the Germans had been defeated and all that remained was a little clearing up. The expansion of the KAR went ahead with speed under Hoskins' direction and it was increased to twenty-two battalions. He asked also that Indian units might remain with him, together with additional artillery. His tenure of command was to be a short one and the Secretary of State for War decided on 3rd May to relieve him of command. He was succeeded by van Deventer who had been in South Africa on sick leave. The intense rains had brought the campaign to a standstill, particularly in the valleys. This presented problems for both sides.

Lettow Vorbeck, in the early part of 1917, was becoming alarmed by the difficulty of feeding and clothing his force: 'more dangerous than the enemy seemed to me the material position of our men.' The supply and baking of bread, so important to the Europeans in his force, was becoming increasingly difficult. There was a great shortage of boots, but Lettow Vorbeck's experiments had proved that a European could go barefoot where there were tolerable paths, but never through the bush. 'To be ready for any emergency, I had some lessons in boot making. It is very convenient for a European who knows the simplest rudiments of this craft to be able to kill an antelope and make a boot from his skin a few days later without the help of any of the tools of civilization.' Such was the man who had held together for three years the German Colonial Army in East Africa.

The heavy rains continued. The British had been actively patrolling, but they had not registered that the Germans were pulling back. The search for fertile areas from which to feed his army was the German commander's main aim, and it involved continual moving. Van Deventer, now in command, decided that Kilwa and Lindi were to form the firm base from which the new Allied offensive would take shape. The 1st Division was re-designated the Kilwa Force and its two brigades became No 1 Column under Colonel Orr and No 2 Column under Colonel Grant. The lack of transport prevented van Deventer

South African 13-pounders at Mtama near Lindi

from launching his attack immediately, but the temporary commander at Kilwa, Brigadier-General Beves, was instructed to push out his column and attack while the Lindi force was told to contain the Germans and build up its strength before attempting any advance.

On 6th July a severe action took place at Mnindi and the Germans withdrew to Narungombe and prepared carefully sited defensive positions. The British columns were to assault left, right and also frontally simultaneously. The German defences were well prepared and held by eight companies and forty-eight machine guns. All columns attacked, but without a great deal of success, for the new KAR recruits were finding conditions hard. Most of the men in the 3rd KAR detachment were seeing action for the first time and the battalion gave way under the stress. The German commander saw this immediately and vigorously counterattacked. This prompt action forced the British column back.

As darkness was falling the Germans mounted another counterattack which had been under preparation for some time. The KAR held this attack and then advanced at the charge, forcing the Germans from their trenches at the bayonet point. The Germans left behind a machine gun which later was to stand for years outside the main barrack gates of the 3rd KAR in Kenya and now stands outside the gates of the 3rd Battalion The Kenya Rifles. This assault by the 3rd KAR changed the whole situation. The Germans withdrew from the other positions and the battle of Narungombe was won, becoming one of the battle honours borne by the KAR.

The British assault from Lindi and Kilwa was planned for September and both forces were strengthened. An airfield was constructed and food dumps built up. In the meantime the Lindi force had attempted some offensive actions, but these had not been too successful. The commander at Lindi, Brigadier-General O'Grady, ordered the 2nd KAR to march out of Lindi and make contact with Lettow Vorbeck's columns coming southwards. At the first encounter the Germans were surprised and were driven back, but eventually counterattacked with over 400 rifles. The engagement was broken off at dusk, but the new KAR battalion had sustained casualties.

The Official History describes the encounter: 'Through pouring rain the battalion marched wearily back through the darkness, having lost three officers out of eight, eight African ranks killed, fifty-four wounded and six missing.' After this episode a lull followed on the Lindi front. O'Grad, was not a man to be beaten and very soon he was again pressing forward to join up with the Kilwa Force. Lettow Vorbeck had moved Wahle across from Mahenge so the German forces outside Lindi were strong. Sensing O'Grady's advance he himself commanded a counterattack. The 2nd KAR came in for very rough handling by Lettow Vorbeck and his askaris. The thick bush afforded the Germans the opportunity to slip round to the rear of the KAR and the British column became isolated. During the night the Germans attacked, the order was given to dig in and the 2nd KAR and the 25th Fusiliers held on.

The position they occupied was far from comfortable, and the following account by an officer in the 25th Fusiliers speaks for itself of the difficulties endured by this battalion: 'It was decided that we were to hold on here, and arrangements were made to bring water, while bully and biscuit would be on ration – no tea, no cooked food, for no fire could be allowed. For five days we lay in the confined square in our shallow trenches, drinking sparingly of foul water. Our porters had a bad time here. At the end of five days many of them were almost unable to walk.'

It is interesting to note the sense of comradeship that sprung up between the KAR and the 25th Fusiliers, adequately described by a Fusilier officer: 'It was here that one saw, and realised, the full fighting courage to which well trained native troops can rise. The First/Second King's African Rifles was one of the original prewar battalions, and magnificently they fought here; and we, who were an Imperial unit, felt that we could not have wished for a stouter, nor a more faithful regiment to fight alongside.'

Van Deventer moved his tactical HQ to Kilwa to co-ordinate the southward advance and the link-up between the Kilwa and Lindi Forces. The two forces were such a short distance from each other, but could they hold Lettow Vorbeck? A decisive movement was impending. Lettow Vorbeck realised this, and, always ready to exploit a tactical weakness, he moved forward with five companies, taking command himself of the operations.

British 4.5-inch howitzers concentrate at Lindi

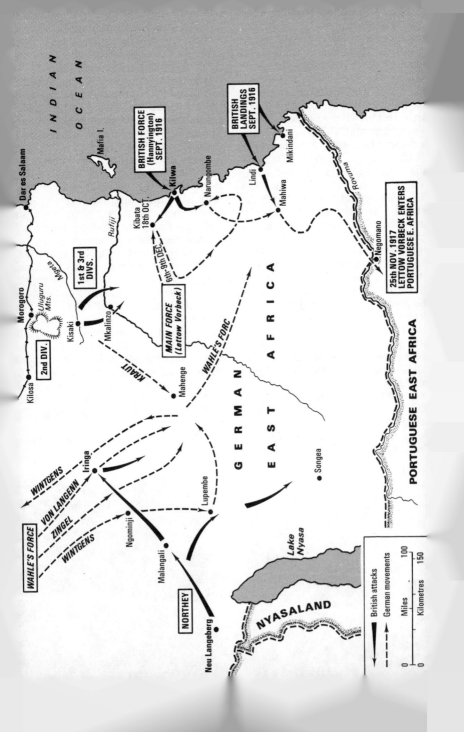

INDIAN OCEAN

Dar es Salaam

Mafia I.

BRITISH FORCE (Hannyington) SEPT. 1916

BRITISH LANDINGS SEPT. 1916

Kilwa

Narungombe

Lindi

Mikindani

Mahiwa

Kibata 18th OCT.

6th-9th DEC.

Negomano

Rovuma

25th NOV. 1917 LETTOW VORBECK ENTERS PORTUGUESE E. AFRICA

Rufiji

Morogoro

Uluguru Mts.

Mgeta

1st & 3rd DIVS.

Kisaki

Mkalinzo

MAIN FORCE (Lettow Vorbeck)

Mahenge

2nd DIV.

Kilosa

KRAUT

WAHLE'S FORC

G E R M A N   E A S T   A F R I C A

P O R T U G U E S E   E A S T   A F R I C A

WINTGENS

Iringa

Lupembe

Songea

VON LANGENN

ZINGEL

Ngominji

WINTGENS

WAHLE'S FORCE

Malangali

NORTHEY

Neu Langeberg

Lake Nyasa

NYASALAND

British attacks

German movements

Miles   100

Kilometres   150

0

Above: The Nigerian Brigade on the march to Mahiwa where, in one of the bitterest engagements of the war, the British forces were badly mauled by the numerically much smaller Germans in October 1917. Below: The Kashmir Mountain Battery get into position at Mahiwa. Lettow Vorbeck's casualties in the battle were high too, and he was forced to evacuate the German colony and invade Portuguese East Africa

The subsequent action was the battle of Mahiwa, one of the bitterest engagements of the war. Attack and counterattack followed in quick succession. The full fire power of the machine gun was exploited. The History of the KAR vividly describes the battle. 'Early in the action all the machine guns of 1/2 KAR were disabled and practically all the gun teams were wiped out. 'C' Company dashed out to recover one gun that had apparently been abandoned in the open, and found the entire team lying dead around it. 'A' and 'B' Companies had been the first committed to battle, and when they were forced to fall back, 'C' Company went through them at the double with bayonets fixed. By the early afternoon the whole battalion was again committed, two companies of 3/2 KAR in support. The whole force remained on the defensive until the enemy broke the attack about 8 pm, 1/2 KAR had lost over half its European and over a third of its African personnel.'

Lettow Vorbeck was in command of this engagement himself. Originally he had intended to execute a flanking movement and catch the British in the rear, but he soon appreciated that the British general was using the same tactics as he had at the Battle of Reata (11th March 1916), that is, throwing his men into action regardless of loss of life on a frontal attack. The German commander strengthened his centre by bringing Wahle and his companies into the middle and, as he says, 'I thought it expedient to increase the disadvantages that the enemy was bringing upon himself by his costly frontal attack and used all my available strength in such a way that the enemy by the increasing fierceness of his frontal attack was bleeding himself to death.'

On the second night of the battle both sides withdrew, the battle had been fought to a standstill and the losses were heavy for it had been fought over open ground. Time was now needed to reorganise, and this applied to both sides. But Lettow Vorbeck considered it was a decisive victory.

'On the evening of 18 October we had, with some 1,500 men, completely defeated a whole enemy detachment of at least 4,000 and probably not less than 6,000 strong. With the exception of Tanga, it was the most serious defeat he had suffered.' British casualties at this battle were about 3,000 men, which was more than 50%. The Germans lost ninety-five killed and 400 wounded. This loss really took the offensive power out of Lettow Vorbeck's army and it was impossible to replace these experienced soldiers or follow up the victory that he had won. During October the British forces from Lindi and Kilwa joined forces and any escape to the west was blocked by Northey's force. He had no alternative but to go southwards nearer the border and the River Rovuma.

In October the German commander assessed the situation and realised that his supply of food would last only for six weeks. At a conference he said 'I firmly stated my opinion that, in spite of all difficulties of supply which must shortly arise in German East Africa, the war could and must be carried on. This could only be done by evacuating German East Africa and invading Portuguese East Africa.'

This invincible German commander was still keeping his aim in mind, after all the hard years' fighting, and now that he had virtually evacuated the German colony he was planning to continue the campaign from Portuguese territory. He skilfully pulled back his force to the River Rovuma. This presented a particular difficulty as Wahle's force was under continual pressure from the advancing British columns. Lettow Vorbeck's aim during November was to get the British columns to close in and concentrate, for this would then give him the ability to move in whatever direction he pleased. He was further

pressured by his lack of ammunition, which would not be sufficient to enable this style of bush warfare to continue, and also the continuous supply problem.

The decision was simple: to reduce his force to about 2,000 rifles and cross into Portugese East Africa. This meant leaving behind considerable numbers of Europeans and Africans who had fought all this way with the commander. It meant that the new force would be totally independent of supply dumps and rely on what it could capture. The German commander's thoughts are well illustrated. 'If we succeeded, however, in maintaining the force in the new territory, the increased independence and mobility used with determination against the less mobile enemy would give us a local superiority in spite of the great numerical superiority of the enemy. The enemy would be compelled to keep an enormous amount of men and material continually on the move and to exhaust his strength to a greater extent proportionately than ourselves.'

The Germans marched down the Rovuma with 300 Europeans, 1,700 askaris and 3,000 carriers. It was difficult for Lettow Vorbeck to re-organise his force on the move. The askaris had been selected because

Indian troops in the Rovuma area, in pursuit of Lettow Vorbeck who had crossed into Portuguese territory in November 1917. German East Africa was now completely in British hands, but the German force had survived and was still tying down large numbers of British troops

they were fit, but they may not necessarily have been experienced. On 25th November 1917 his small army crossed the River Rovuma at Negomano into Portuguese East Africa. Not all his force managed to cross the river and some detachments were left behind. The largest was under the command of Captain Tafel. It eventually surrendered. German East Africa was now in British hands, but the campaign was by no means finished. In fact it had entered only another phase, but the service chiefs in Whitehall were convinced that the struggle had been drawn to a successful conclusion. The Allied commander, van Deventer, assessed the situation accurately: 'an equally arduous campaign though on a very much smaller scale will, however, probably still be necessary before the German force in Portuguese East Africa is finally brought to book, for the country is vast and communications are difficult.'

Surrender,
but not defeat

Before van Deventer could invade Portuguese East Africa and pursue Lettow Vorbeck he had to reorganise his force. Fortunately for him the rains were again imminent and the necessary respite was obtained, during which time all Indian troops were sent home and the British continued the campaign largely with African troops. On 1st July 1917 the KAR totalled 535 officers, 118 British NCOs and 23,325 Africans, but by 1st July 1918 it had been increased to 1,193 officers, 1,497 British NCOs and 30,658 Africans.

Van Deventer decided his tasks were firstly to fight the Germans whenever and wherever he could in a war of attrition, secondly to prevent them invading Nyasaland and finally to prevent them attempting a return into German East Africa. A force was formed under the command of Lieutenant-Colonel Giffard, known as 'Kartucol' with the aim of preventing the Germans returning back into their colony. Another force was founded and its main lines of attack were to come from the sea. The Gold Coast Regiment were the first to land at Porto Amelia in December. Later it was joined by the 4th KAR, known as

Lettow Vorbeck's advance through Portuguese East Africa. Normally the column marched for six hours a day, with a half-hour halt every two hours, covering fifteen-twenty miles per day

The bearers were taught to march at the same speed as the askaris

'Rosecol'. Eventually this force was expanded by the addition of 'Kartucol' and redesignated 'Pamforce'.

Lettow Vorbeck for his part was quick to assume the offensive, and almost immediately crossed the Rovuma. A small Portuguese outpost was seized at Negomano. The surprised Portuguese put up very little fight and the German askaris were very soon attacking with such vigour that they got completely out of control; as Lettow Vorbeck said, 'It was a fearful melée.' It was an important engagement, if somewhat small, for here the German forces were able to capture valuable medical stores, rifles, six machine guns, thirty horses and much ammunition. It was also a fortunate engagement for Lettow Vorbeck so early on in this phase of the war. 'With one blow we had freed ourselves of a great part of our difficulties.' The ever present difficulty over food supplies dictated his route; the River Lugenda was the obvious direction. To keep control of a column marching over vast distances with nearly 3,000 carriers with the

constant anxiety of brushing against the enemy exercised his ability to command and control to the limit.

The bearers, women and children, were all taught to march at the same speed as the askaris, but a half-hour halt was called every two hours and the column marched for six hours a day, covering approximately fifteen to twenty miles. The command was divided by Lettow Vorbeck into groups of three companies, with a supply detachment and a field hospital each. The advanced guard carried the bulk of the machine guns, with the following companies a reasonable distance behind. In this way the essential factor of balance was always maintained. On account of this good tactical balance, the column was able to react immediately to the unexpected. To obtain reasonable quantities of food for his column he decided to split it up again, and so Wahle pushed inland to the west.

Lettow Vorbeck's generalship was often marked by his ready ability to detach part of his force under subordinate commanders and give them a completely free hand within the overall framework of his plan. Indeed, a great deal of his success in his mobile defence can be attributed to his willingness to delegate responsibility to his subordinate commanders. With the absence of modern communications it must be appreciated that these actions took considerable courage on the commander's part, but usually it paid great dividends and possibly the only example of failure was in the case of Captain Tafel who surrendered to the British just after Lettow Vorbeck had crossed into Portuguese East Africa. The fault lay in lack of communications. Tafel thought Lettow Vorbeck had been captured.

'I was straightaway put upon the rack by the news ... During the march up the Lugenda when we had to keep the different detachments and companies further apart in order to facilitate the search for food, it was necessary to impress upon subordinate leaders the importance of keeping the whole force in touch. It was, however, not to be expected that these officers, who later performed such excellent work as leaders of detachments and worked so successfully in co-operation with the rest, should possess the necessary training from the beginning.' Full well did Lettow Vorbeck realise the problems he was making by detaching parts of his force away from the main body, but the pressure of finding sufficient supplies was his continual burden. With this in mind he detached Captain Göring and Captain Koehle to the more fertile river valleys in search of food.

During this phase of the operations his forces were well dispersed looking for food. Good supplies were found in the Medo region, and accordingly the bulk of the force was pulled into the east. The marches, as always during the rainy season, were great feats of endurance. Lettow Vorbeck himself was not well. 'In torrential rain we marched east. The usually dry ravines had become raging torrents. The mule I was riding on account of fever – I am apparently very sensitive

to malaria, from which I suffered a great deal – as well as the few other riding animals that had not found their way into the cooking pot, swam across.'

While the rainy season was in full swing the British were trying to reorganise their forces. They had received a congratulatory telegram from George V: 'I heartily congratulate you and the troops under your command on having driven the remaining forces of the enemy out of German East Africa.' But nobody was really sure whether the war was over or not. The pursuit into Portuguese East Africa would present enormous problems for the British forces as their resupply base was at Dar es Salaam on the coast. The lines of communication would become impossibly stretched.

Meanwhile the British advance inland from Porto Amelia was continuing slowly. The plan was to advance with two columns and take Medo from the south. It was not until April that force 'Rosecol' came close to Koehl's detachment at Medo The plan was simple. 'Rosecol' was to attack Medo frontally while 'Kartucol' went on a flanking move to the left and approached from the south. The Germans had prepared a good defensive position in Medo, and the British attack very soon came under effective machine gun fire as the Germans counterattacked. The British force was very short of ammunition and bayonets were fixed to repel the attack. Great feats of gallantry were performed by the KAR on this day. A certain Lance-Corporal Sovera, DCM, of the 2nd KAR climbed a tree with his Lewis gun and brought very effective fire to bear on the German positions. 'Later on, Sovera took command of a section that had become shaky after losing its NCO, he then danced an *Ngoma* (African dance) up and down the firing line to hearten his men.'

The British advance continued towards Nanunga and Northey's force in

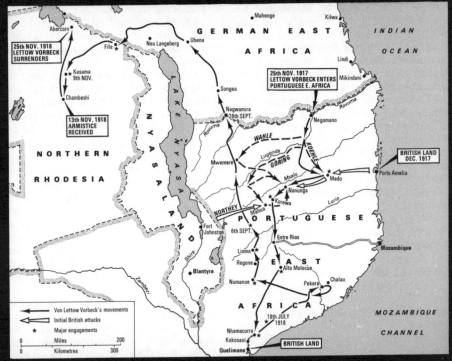

Lettow Vorbeck's marauding in Portuguese East Africa during 1918

Within the map:

GERMAN EAST AFRICA

INDIAN OCEAN

25th NOV. 1918
LETTOW VORBECK
SURRENDERS

Abercorn

Fife

Neu Langeberg

Ubena

Mahenge

Kilwa

Lindi

25th NOV. 1917
LETTOW VORBECK ENTERS
PORTUGUESE E. AFRICA

Mikindani

Kasama
9th NOV.

Chambeshi

Songea

Nagwamira
28th SEPT.

Rovuma

Negomano

13th NOV. 1918
ARMISTICE
RECEIVED

NORTHERN

RHODESIA

NYASALAND

LAKE NYASA

Rovuma

WAHLE

Mwemere

Lugenda

GORING

KOEHLS

BRITISH LAND
DEC. 1917

Msalu

Nanunga

Medo

Porto Amelia

NORTHEY

Mahua

Korewa

Lurio

PORTUGUESE

Fort Johnston

6th SEPT.

Shire

Entre Rios

Mozambique

Liomo

EAST

Regone

Alto Molocue

Blantyre

Numanoe

Pekera

Chalau

Zambezi

AFRICA

18th JULY
1918

MOZAMBIQUE

CHANNEL

Nhamacurra

Kokosani

BRITISH LAND

Quelimane

Legend:

Von Lettow Vorbeck's movements

Initial British attacks

★ Major engagements

0   Miles   200

0   Kilometres   300

the west pushed across to Mahua; hopes were raised and it was thought possible that the German column might be encircled and captured. But Lettow Vorbeck had yet again skilfully pulled back his force on Nanunga and drawn in all his detachments, proceeding south-west in search of more food. For his force the food situation had become critical again; maize had to be artificially ripened by drying it.

The British advanced from Nanunga towards Korewa and their advance guard surprised the German column eating their midday meal. The surprise was followed up by a quick flank attack. The Germans could not withdraw in their normal way and lost a great deal of ammunition (100,000 rounds) and money. This quick engagement brought to an end the first phase of the campaign in Portuguese East Africa. Lettow Vorbeck had managed again to extricate his forces, but the British from Porto Amelia and the west had now joined forces. He was forced to go south. He reproached himself for the action at Korewa. 'Unfortunately I omitted to give Koehl's detachment definite orders to withdraw their main force immediately from the unfavourable country... instead of a positive order, I gave him instructions which left him too much freedom of action.'

Van Deventer's plan was now to fortify a line of towns across Portuguese East Africa, from Porto Amelia through Medo , Mahua and Fort Johnston, aimed at preventing the Germans from doubling back northwards. He then pressed the pursuit with all possible vigour. The Gold Coast Regiment was detailed to hold the line of fortified posts and the 2nd KAR took up the pursuit.

The advance was resumed on 24th May, and the British forces pressed forward 'daily in a monotonous series of seemingly endless marches, interspersed with minor actions against a rear guard that never stood for long.' The Germans moved to the country around Entre Rios (formerly Malema) which was incredibly fertile, but Lettow Vorbeck decided that his stay in this area would not be for long.

'I decided gradually to evacuate the region, in spite of its extraordinary fertility and slip through the ring in which the enemy columns were enclosing me in the fertile district of the Malema River. My idea was that a small part of my troops should hold off these enemy columns and keep them so busy that they would think they were involved in a serious affair and attack my rearguard properly.' The British were once again faced by the twin problems of Lettow Verbeck's tactics and their own lack of food supplies. The ration convoy took days to get forward to the fighting troops, and on one occasion when it arrived there was only coffee for the Europeans! They had to subsist on African rations of sweet potatoes, rice and mealie flour. During this period of the campaign troops were far worse off as regards rations than at any other time.

The tactics that Lettow Vorbeck hoped to put into practice were not always possible. The British had been caught once before at Korewa and had no intention of making the same mistake. Their plan was, on making contact, to push out a detachment which would then work round to the rear of the German position, but, as Lettow Vorbeck realised, if he put his force in depth the British outflanking movement could find itself cut off and opposed by greater numbers. Putting any tactics into effect in the dense bush was extremely difficult, and when contact was made it was often impossible to tell who was friend and who was foe.

On one occasion Lieutenant von Ruckteschell, who was pulling back from a rearguard action, came across a British outflanking detachment who thought the Germans were friends. The lieutenant carefully put his machine guns into position and then opened up at point blank range. Always Lettow Vorbeck kept in mind the necessity of obtaining further supplies and ammunition. The Portugese settlement of Alto Molocue appeared a likely source, for a captured map had revealed that it was the base of a garrison of over company strength. The essential element was surprise, for he was determined to capture the ammunition. The situation strategically was rather comical: the Germans chased the Portuguese and the British chased the Germans.

Alto Molocue was captured according to plan, together with numerous maps and documents which gave the Germans a good idea of what to expect nearer Quelimane. It was concluded that the area to the south contained plenty of supplies of all kinds. The Portuguese had unfortunately slipped out of Alto Molocue with their ammunition, so Lettow Vorbeck very quickly despatched follow-up patrols to locate and seize the escaping Portuguese supplies. Various Portuguese patrols were captured and a considerable amount of food, but still not the ammunition which by this time was becoming vital.

Lettow Vorbeck's rapid advance southwards forced van Deventer to shift the emphasis of his force southwards. He transferred his base post from Porto Amelia to Mozambique and the whole operational area was shifted to the south, for it was not now considered necessary to hold the Rovuma line. Van Deventer also decided to land forces at Quelimane to reinforce the Portuguese garrison already there.

Lettow Vorbeck pushed further southwards towards Quelimane with Captain Müller's detachment leading. The German commander always travelled well forward, but not so far forward that he was unable to influence any unforeseen incident with the reserves. Müller made for Kokosani and Nhamacurra where many African informers confirmed the location of supplies, weapons and ammunition. On arrival at Kokosani, Müller executed a flanking movement which took the Portuguese garrison by surprise and he captured two Portuguese field guns and a number of rifles, but still the ammunition stores were not located.

Kokosani was a considerable town with factories and a railway, and Lettow Vorbeck was sure that the valuable ammunition stores that he so badly needed would be in this area. He appreciated that the ammunition would be near the railway and not in the factories, so on 1st July he turned his reluctant columns about and they retraced their steps along the railway towards Nhamacurra. Very soon the head of the column came under rapid fire and was pinned to the ground. The German commander decided that a frontal attack would achieve nothing, although some well-aimed artillery and machine gun fire might achieve a measure of success. Daylight was nearly over so the Germans maintained contact but did not attack until the following day. Müller by this time had several larger guns in working order and over 200 shells that he had captured on the previous day. The artillery bombardment started from a very short range and its effect was instant. The first shells caused panic among the Portuguese troops in Nhamacurra, and these troops holding the forward trenches pulled back in chaos. Müller seized this opportunity and charged forward.

The remainder of the position held by KAR troops became untenable, and Major Gore-Browne in command had no alternative but to pull back. The only line of retreat was along the river, and the British attempted to find a ford. Unable to do this, a disaster followed which is well described by Lettow Vorbeck: 'Our flying foes reached the river Nhamacurra which ran immediately behind their positions, quickly pulled off their boots and dashed into the water. Here most of the hostile troops were drowned, including their commander Major Gore-Browne.' The withdrawal had become a rout and the British forces sustained large casualties. At Nhamacurra Lettow Vorbeck found what he was looking for, vast supplies of ammunition. The backward trek had been worth it. The factory was full of sugar, clothing and medical supplies, and quantities of ammunition were located everywhere. The Germans also captured 350 modern British and Portuguese rifles and were able to discard the old 1871 pattern rifles completely. Lettow Vorbeck's small command was now equipped to wage war for some time to come. He had achieved his aim again.

Van Deventer's reaction was to order all his columns to converge on Nhamacurra, but Lettow Vorbèck was not going to be captured quite so easily. He realised that the British would be worried about the port of Quelimane, and consequently he wanted to give the impression that he was making for this port. He then intended to push north-east towards Mozambique and so force the British columns to double back northwards, thereby exhausting themselves in long marches.

The situation that developed now was almost comic, Lettow Vorbeck and the *Schutztruppe* were pushing northwards and all the British columns were going southwards. The inevitable happened and on 18th July a KAR column ran headlong into the German forces. A fire fight rapidly developed and the CO of the KAR, Colonel Dickenson, was captured and many of his officers killed. Dickenson, now a prisoner, spent the rest of the war marching with Lettow Vorbeck's column. He and Lettow Vorbeck became firm friends. (It is unfortunate to recall that Colonel Dickenson died of Spanish Flu in Dar es Salaam at the end of the war, having survived all the perils of the marching).

Lettow Vorbeck's column by this time had grown quite large. He had collected numerous British and Portuguese prisoners, but for the latter he had little or no admiration: 'It was interesting to notice that the English prisoners whom we took with us, for the most part, accepted as a matter of course the hardships of the long marches, the constant crossing of rivers and the countless difficulties connected with supplies and transport. It was quite otherwise with the Portuguese officers. It was true they were in an unenviable position; for the most part they were infected with syphilis and were carefully avoided by the English prisoners.'

The German commander now pushed northwards to Pequerra and during August van Deventer regrouped his forces with the intention of preventing him from going northwards by making a firm base along the Mozambique-Entre Rios road. The British were thoroughly confused, for really they had had no indication of his intentions. The German commander held the initiative. It was just a question of deciding which way to go. To him it was obvious that patrols and columns were converging on Chalaua from various directions. His intention now was to march westwards towards Blantyre or east of Lake Nyasa. The morale of the German force was still very high. The supplies from Nhamacurra were becoming scarce but he still managed to hold his remarkable force together.

The description of a halt during the march indicates very clearly the German commander's attitude and the morale of his men: 'During a halt we lunched in the congenial company of Lieutenant Ott, Sergeant-Major Nordenholz and other officers of the advanced guard. We had long grown accustomed during the halts to bring out, without ceremony, a piece of bread and a box of lard or hippopotamus fat. As soon as a halt was called every black would bring out his lunch. It was very jolly when the whole force bivouacked in this way in the forest, in the best of spirits and refreshed themselves for fresh exertions, fresh marches and fresh fighting.' After four years of outstanding exertion, the

German commander's drive and enthusiasm was still as forceful as ever in spite of the fact that he suffered continually from malaria and had recently nearly lost the sight of one of his eyes.

Continuing the advance towards Numanoe Lettow Vorbeck's leading company made contact with the 4th KAR. The latter, realising that the German strength was considerable, pulled back into Numanoe itself and conducted a successful delaying action. The Germans attacked Numanoe from the rear. The British force was defeated and their CO was taken prisoner. Once again Lettow Vorbeck obtained supplies, and something in the order of 40,000 rounds of ammunition were captured.

The next town on his route northwards was Regone, but he had captured documents which indicated that the British were defending Regone in strength so he chose to avoid this strongpoint. At this juncture in the march he had to decide which way to continue. He had originally intended to go westwards but felt that by now the British would have a considerable advantage because, controlling Lake Nyasa, they would be able to concentrate their troops quickly. Therefore to continue the march westwards was ruled out. To go northwards would certainly surprise the British and Lettow Vorbeck reasoned that a northward thrust would indicate to the British that he was aiming for Tabora. It was then possible that the British would take the bulk of their army by sea from Portuguese East East Africa to Dar es Salaam and then by rail to Tabora. He therefore concluded that he would point northwards in the direction of Tabora but then turn westwards when he had reached the end of Lake Nyasa.

He was making the British dance to his tune. Wherever he went, they followed – an object lesson in guerrilla tactics. It can be imagined how this inconclusive wandering about the Portuguese territory made heavy demands on the British supply system. The British columns chasing Lettow Vorbeck very soon outstripped their supply backing and many were time and time again reduced to starvation rations. It was possible in Portuguese East Africa to buy food from the local Africans, but the method of payment became a problem because silver was scarce and this seemed to be the only thing the Africans would accept. Cloth from Zanzibar was used as a currency for quite some time, but eventually all the African women had enough of this and something else had to be used. In the German banks in Dar es Salaam there were quantities of silver which the British had confiscated and melted down and then used as currency in Portuguese East Africa.

Some British forces attempted to live off the country as the Germans did. This was partially successful, and it certainly made them completely independent of the supply base. Nevertheless the bulk of the British army was tied to its supply system. The success of Lettow Vorbeck's force must be measured by the vast number of British troops it kept in the field and also by the vast amount of supplies it diverted from the more important theatres of war. His overall aim, declared in 1914, was just that: to divert British war effort from Europe to East Africa. He was fulfilling one of the classic principles of guerrilla warfare, a small mobile force tying down vast numbers of men and material.

The advance northwards continued. Lettow Vorbeck avoided the British defensive position at Regone and pushed on towards Lioma. His advance detachments located the British whom they observed digging in and

The columns move through the widely varying topography of the huge Portuguese territory – savannah, forest, bush – often dressed in captured British and Portuguese uniforms as their own wore out and could not be replaced

finally preparing their defensive positions. Immediately the Germans attacked. The British defenders were the 1st KAR who were taken completely unawares by the German attack and lost a complete platoon in consequence. Very quickly, however, the KAR counterattacked and soon the the Germans were withdrawing. But their commander had committed them too far and they suffered casualties. The guerrilla force must always avoid direct confrontation with the stronger enemy; Lettow Vorbeck nearly always managed this, but on this occasion he had difficulty in controlling the battle. During this engagement he lost seventeen Europeans and about 200 askaris. The command problem in this kind of engagement in the bush is very difficult.

He describes his actions: 'In the late afternoon I was astonished to notice that the rest of the troops had not followed the detachments of Müller and Göring but were marching along the valley to our right. In order to bring the force together, I tried to descend from my hill. The descent, however, proved impossible; the rocks were steep, almost perpendicular. Fortunately there was another small path. This we succeeded in climbing down. Even here it was very steep in places but the bare feet of the carriers gave them a good foothold and I too, after taking off my boots, managed the descent. It was pitch dark and we had no water. At last, however, we found some and a load fell from my heart when we came upon the rest of the force.' For a commander forty-eight years old and completing his fourth year in these trying conditions in East Africa this was indeed a great physical performance.

The British had now concentrated their columns and were following up quickly, giving him no time for rest and the all-important task of food gathering. But it must be remembered that the British would have difficulty in living off the land that he had passed through because it would

have clearly been devastated by him. The direct pursuit northwards was left to 'Kartucol'. But the commander changed his tactics. As soon as his advanced guard hit the Germans they fired from the hip and advanced forward. This was successful and the German rearguard withdrew more rapidly. It is interesting to note that in Europe a young German commander, Captain Erwin Rommel, was using the same tactics, and with similar success.

On 6th September in the northwards advance the British leading elements overtook the German main body, so Lettow Vorbeck immediately attacked. The fighting fell mainly on the 2nd Company of the 2nd Regiment 2nd KAR. All officers were wounded and the CSM only just managed to get the company back to join up with the main column. The Germans concentrated their force and attacked vigorously. The situation was critical, for the British vanguard was well spread out and ran the risk of being defeated in detail By this time the 1st Regiment KAR were two miles and the 3rd Regiment KAR four miles away. The 2nd Regiment took heavy punishment from the German force and lost the the bulk of its British officers and NCOs either killed or wounded. But Lettow Vorbeck did not push home his attack with his reserves. To become committed to a pitched battle with a strong enemy is not the guerrilla commander's aim. Nevertheless this sharp engagement stopped the British from continuing their advance; 'Kartucol' was unable to continue. Another column called 'Shortcol' was brought forward to carry on. What was left of the 1st Regiment was taken out of the line and put in reserve.

The German force now numbered 176 Europeans and 1,487 askaris. This small efficient force moved northwards again but this time without any close pursuit. Another enemy struck them – influenza swept through the force, about half had bronchial catarrh and from three to six men in each company had inflammation of the lungs and as it was only possible for some eighty sick to be carried in the whole force, about twenty men suffering with inflammation of the lungs had to march at times. Yet again this great commander held his force together and pushed on towards German East Africa. On 28th September 1918 he reached the River Rovuma at Nagwamira and crossed back into German East Africa. The small guerrilla force rested for a few days, enjoying the plentiful good food. But soon their commander had them marching forward, for he was continuing the campaign.

The initiative still lay with him. Van Deventer was forced to redeploy his forces. A new organisation was formed, called 'Cenforce'. 'Kartucol', after its pursuit of 1,600 miles through the forests and swamps of Portuguese East Africa, was broken up. It is to the great credit of the German leader that he was still able to dictate to the British (who had overwhelming forces) the future lines of the campaign. He now moved northwards to Songea, rich in cattle and farm produce. The health and morale of the German force was once again at its normal high level. It is interesting to note that the German force still had one of the *Königsberg*'s guns with it. This artillery piece had been manhandled over this fantastic journey by Lieutenant Wenig and his team.

The British operations now fell upon two of the Uganda regiments of the 4th KAR. The 2nd Regiment marched to Fort Johnston on Lake Nyasa. It was in a desperate state when it arrived at the lake, for it had been fighting since March with no issues of clothing. It embarked on boats and moved northwards up Lake Nyasa and then to Songea. This regiment joined up with the Northern Rhodesian Police and continued the pursuit of Lettow Vorbeck's columns.

Lettow Vorbeck decided now to move westwards instead of going due north towards Tabora. This decision was made mainly because food supplies were plentiful in Rhodesia. At Ubena he left Wahle who was now sick. About this time Lettow Vorbeck captured some newspapers and learned that Cambrai had fallen and hostilities had ceased in Bulgaria. Armentières had also fallen, but he wrote 'positions could be given up for so many different reasons and I did not attribute any decisive importance to this news.' The small German army in East Africa would continue to fight.

The German column moved towards Isoka where it was appreciated that the British held a valuable supply base. At this point van Deventer was again forced to change his plans. The 1st Regiment of the 2nd KAR were moved south from Tabora to Bismarckburg. The 1st Regiment of the 4th KAR was moved up Lake Nyasa to Neu Langenberg and the Northern Rhodesian Police marched towards Isoka. Lettow Vorbeck's column completed a forced march in ten hours and duly reached its target, Isoka. The German commander was not prepared to attack, but he used his trench mortars against the well prepared defences. This artillery on its own was not successful and he marched on without risking a pitched battle. Pursuer and pursued were now in unknown country. The British advanced guard commander was reading from a small atlas of the world at 200 miles to the inch!

Kasama was to be the next objective. The Germans seized this with little effort on 9th November but unfortunately there was little ammunition to be taken. On 13th November the German force moved southwards to Chambeshi where supplies were expected. Lettow Vorbeck went forward on his bicycle to see for himself. It was on this day that he received news of the Armistice. It was in the form of a telegram from van Deventer.

'13.11.18 To Norforce, Karwinfor via Fife [*Isoka*]. Send following to General von Lettow Vorbeck under white flag. War Office London telegraph that

Clause 17 of Armistice signed by German government provides for unconditional surrender of all German forces operating in East Africa within one month from November 11th. My conditions are; First, hand over all Allied prisoners in your hands; Second, bring your forces to Abercorn without delay. Third, hand over all your arms and ammunition to my representative at Abercorn. I will however allow you and your officers and European ranks to retain their arms for the present in consideration of the gallant fight which you have made, provided that you bring your force to Abercorn without delay. Arrangements will be made at Abercorn to send all Germans to Morogoro and to repatriate German askaris. Kindly send an early answer giving probable date of arrival at Abercorn and numbers of German officers and men, askaris and followers.'

Lettow Vorbeck agreed to the surrender terms and his army (at this time 155 Europeans, 1,168 askaris and 3,000 other Africans) accepted their fate. The army marched by short stages to Abercorn to surrender formally. Lettow Vorbeck did all in his power to see that his men received their back pay, but only paper certificates could be given out because the British refused to find the 1,500,000 rupees that were necessary.

In an article in *The Times* in 1920 Major Hawkins describes the march to Abercorn: 'On the morning of November 6th von Lettow arrived at Kasama and handed in to us his written unconditional surrender, provided the terms turned out to be as represented to him. At midday the whole force marched back through our camp en route to Abercorn, a hundred miles away where the official surrender was to take place . . . von Lettow himself turned out to be a very different man from what we expected. A little over medium height and wearing a short pointed beard, with his hair turning grey, he is a fine looking man of 49. Instead of the haughty Prussian one expected to meet, he turned out to be a most courteous and perfectly mannered man, his behaviour throughout his captivity was a model to anyone in such a position.'

The *Schutztruppe* marched into Abercorn on 25th November 1918 with General Paul von Lettow Vorbeck at the head of the column. Brigadier-General Edwards was on parade to receive the surrender and a guard of honour was provided by the KAR. Lettow Vorbeck marched his men on to the area provided for them, he quickly formed them into three ranks, moved forward a few paces, saluted the British flag and then read out his formal statement of surrender in German. He then repeated in it English, and General Edwards accepted on behalf of His Majesty King George V. All the German officers were then introduced and Lettow Vorbeck was presented to all the British officers.

It is interesting to observe that ex-Governor Schnee was at this surrender parade. He had survived the long and gruelling journey with the *Schutztruppe*. On many occasions he had disagreed with the German general as to the direction of the war effort in the colony. Temperamentally opposed, nevertheless they had been thrown together by the war. Throughout, Schnee had doggedly continued to insist on his nominal rights as C-in-C of the Defence Force. Just as stubbornly, the professional Lettow Vorbeck had continued to ignore them. Initially, as it has been seen, the Governor had attempted to oppose Vorbeck's plans for the defence of the colony; in this, he had been over-ruled by the Berlin government. This setback, however, had not deterred him from continually asserting his authority – somewhat exaggerated and imagined in Lettow Vorbeck's eyes – whenever the opportunity presented itself.

Lettow Vorbeck in a British POW camp. He had surrendered, undefeated, after the Armistice

Now, with his military commander, Dr Schnee was facing the ceremonials of defeat and the bitter moment had come when he witnessed the almost tireless commander order his askaris to lay down their rifles. This being done, they were marched away to be interned. The white members of the German force were allowed to retain their arms. At least the Allies were trying to acknowledge that theirs had been an honourable defeat at the end of a magnificent fight.

By late afternoon the last of the arms had been surrendered and Lettow Vorbeck had signed the necessary surrender documents. In obvious admiration of his exploits as a soldier, the British officers invited him and his officers to dine with them. He refused. He preferred to meet Colonel Dickinson who had shared the trials and fatigues of their forced marches of the past few months as the leader of the Allied prisoners-of-war. During that time captor and captive had become firm friends, bound by the ties of mutual admiration and goodwill which frequently flourished between soldiers on both sides in the First World War.

Then, perhaps true to form, instead of a good dinner with his captors, he went to inspect the camp where the backbone of his army, the German askaris, were interned. He was indignant. Having listened to their loud complaints, he decided that conditions there were intolerable for his troops. Surrounded by a thick hedge of thorn, he considered the camp to be far too small for the numbers of men it contained. Having quietened the askaris, he demanded to see General Edwards with whom he conferred at once, stating that there was no need for him to fear that German soldiers would escape!

The following day, the German contingent proceeded to Bismarckburg on Lake Tanganyika guarded by askaris of the KAR to await the steamers to take them across the lake to Kigoma. The steamers were not ready and the inevitable wait occurred. Lettow Vorbeck complained again: his soldiers were being continually guarded, and he objected to their being treated as prisoners-of-war. His complaint was duly forwarded to the commander who replied on 3rd December that he had no alternative to such treatment until he received contrary instructions from London. Prisoners they were and so they would stay and be treated.

This reply incensed some of the German officers, who, irritated at the waiting around, began to formulate schemes to renew the campaign even at this stage. It was as if they could not believe that defeat had finally overtaken them. Having endured so much together, their faith in and admiration for their commander knew no bounds. He had only to assent and a private army would have come into being. But even Lettow Vorbeck knew this was but a pipe dream. One wonders if he almost wished it were not. This was the spirit he had fostered throughout the four years of war, 'a soldierly spirit, a spirit which did not shrink, even after we had handed over all our arms, from storming an enemy camp and once more procuring for ourselves the means to continue the war.'

Tempers began to fray further, but fortunately the steamers were brought alongside in a little while and the German prisoners were shipped to Kigoma, which was at the head of the rail to Dar es Salaam. Kigoma was now in Belgian hands. Contrary to what they expected (these colonial German officers would appear to have had a guilt complex towards their Belgian counterparts), they were reasonably received by the Belgian officers 'who displayed a tactful re-

Top : Parties of German sick and walking wounded are rounded up for a lengthy internment by the British. *Right :* The last shipload of German prisoners (with Lettow Vorbeck aboard) embarks for Germany from Dar es Salaam on 17th January 1919

serve' towards them and even produced red wine for their meal.

The journey to Tabora was continued by rail, and there they were greeted by a crowd of Germans with ready complaints for the ear of the commander of supposed outrages committed by both occupying Belgian and British troops. The train moved on to Dodoma, staying long enough to allow many of the prisoners to bathe there. At Morogoro some German women they had left behind there in 1916 were waiting to welcome them with tea, coffee, rolls, cakes and fruit. It was like a royal progress.

Dar es Salaam was finally reached on 8th December. Fortunately, there were no complaints about accommodation this time. The Chief of Staff of the British commander, General Sheppard himself, conducted Lettow Vorbeck and Governor Schnee to 'our very pretty house outside the camp.' Van Deventer had sent a lunch over in advance as a welcoming gesture, such was the tremendous admiration of the Allied generals for the German. A car was placed at his disposal which enabled him to move about Dar almost at random with one British officer as escort. He could hardly consider himself a prisoner. The chivalries of war were very much to the fore in 1918. He held many discussions with 'intelligent Englishmen' and was pleased to hear that, like him, they considered that Germany must retain her colonies both on account of her growing population and on the economic

grounds which had originally motivated Karl Peters to conclude his treaties in East Africa. So at least he was reassured that the fight in the German colony had not been in vain.

But Spanish flu' was to prevent him and many of his staff from continuing their discussions with their new British friends. An epidemic swept through the camp and many inmates died. Approximately ten per cent of all the captives succumbed, among them Captain Spangenberg, one of Vorbeck's closest staff officers, as well as Colonel Dickinson, his Allied friend.

Time dragged for Lettow Vorbeck and his men. Repatriation to Germany seemed to be continually delayed. It was not until 17th January 1919 that the German prisoners embarked, with

Berlin, 2nd March 1919. The undefeated general and his men are acclaimed as they ride in triumph through the crowded streets

women and children, on their first stage of their journey homewards.

Via Capetown, their ship reached Rotterdam at the end of February and thence to Germany to a tremendous reception. Lettow Vorbeck arrived to a hero's adulation. The undefeated general had arrived home. On 2nd March 1919 the jubilant crowds of Berlin gave him the welcome he so richly deserved. Mounted on a horse, he was acclaimed as he rode in triumph through the streets of Berlin. A fitting climax to a singular campaign.

The tactics of guerrilla war

No account of the campaign in German East Africa can be complete without an assessment of the generalship of General Paul von Lettow Vorbeck. Although other generals made contributions to this campaign – Smuts, Sheppard and van Deventer – it is Lettow Vorbeck's name that should be primarily remembered. Without his drive and determination the campaign would not have lasted the full four years. It is a campaign which illustrates all the principles of guerrilla war, and is notable as one of the first guerrilla wars in the 20th Century fought with modern weapons.

At the beginning of the war Lettow Vorbeck stated his aim, to bring the war to German East Africa and with his small force encourage the British to send as many men and materials as possible to this minor theatre, thereby depriving the major areas of conflict of badly needed troops. This aim in itself typifies guerrilla activity, a small force holding down a force vastly superior to itself.

During 1914 Lettow Vorbeck's army was on the offensive in East Africa. He concentrated in the north and crossed

A German raiding party, one of the basic units in Lettow Vorbeck's guerrilla tactics. As the British advanced, their lines of communication lengthened and were continually harassed by these small parties of raiders